THE ORIGIN OF WAVES

BOOKS BY AUSTIN CLARKE

FICTION

The Survivors of the Crossing
Amongst Thistles and Thorns
The Meeting Point
Storm of Fortune
The Bigger Light
When He Was Free and Young and He Used to Wear Silks
When Women Rule
The Prime Minister
Nine Men Who Laughed
Proud Empires
In This City
There Are No Elders

NONFICTION

Growing Up Stupid Under the Union Jack
A Passage Back Home

SELECTED WRITINGS

The Austin Clarke Reader

The Origin of Waves

AUSTIN CLARKE

M&S

Canadian Cataloguing in Publication Data

Clarke, Austin, 1934 –
    The origin of waves

ISBN 0-7710-2127-5

I. Title.

PS8505.L38O74 1997   C813'.54   C96-932212-7
PR9199.3.C52O74 1997

The publishers acknowledge the support of the Canada Council and the Ontario Arts Council for their publishing program.

Quotation on p. vii from "Prelude" in *Rights of Passage* by Edward Brathwaite, Oxford University Press, 1967. Reprinted by permission.

Typesetting by M&S, Toronto
Printed and bound in Canada

McClelland & Stewart Inc.
The Canadian Publishers
481 University Avenue
Toronto, Ontario
M5G 2E9

1 2 3 4 5 6   02 01 00 99 98 97

For Denise

"Memories are smoke
lips we can't kiss
hands we can't hold
will never be
enough for us;
for we have learned
to live with sun
with sin
with soil
with rock . . ."

> – Edward Brathwaite, "Prelude, "
> *Rights of Passage*

"Then let not winter's ragged hand deface
In thee thy summer ere thou be distilled:
Make sweet some vial: treasure thou some place
With beauty's treasure, ere it be self-killed."

> – Shakespeare, Sonnet Nº6

We were sitting on the sand. The sand on the beach was the same colour as the shell of the conch. The conch was empty, dead and old. Its pink insides, so delicious and crunchy when half-raw, were eaten years ago. Its shell reminded me of its sweet taste. And it had been thrown back into the sea, from which it had floated back onto the sand, like the flotsam and the jetsam of the sea, and for days now, perhaps months, it lay on the sand, like an unused instrument. It could have been years. On this afternoon, we just watched the conch-shell, as the waves came in and covered it, and changed its colour for just one moment, and then the waves hid it from our sight two times. Once, when the wave brought the sand in its thrust, making the wave look like Cream of Wheat, and once again, the second dying time, when the wave went back out to sea, without the sand on its back, the conch-shell was hardly moved from its stubborn and insistent posture of voicelessness. Sometimes, when we were at home, a few hundred yards from the beach where our fathers and uncles had sat before us, and at night, especially on dark nights when their tales matched the heaviness of the night and their memories, they would remember a fisherman who had been dragged up from this same beach, filled with water, drowned and blue; and how someone had put this same conch-shell to his lips, and had blown a signal, a tune, a warning of things to come, and sounded the declaration of the tragedy. And the entire village would come out to mourn.

We were sitting on the same sand where our fathers and uncles used to sit in the long storytelling nights of accidents at sea, and of women they had loved. And sometimes, of women who loved them back, and of women who had died before their declaration of love. When the waves sped back into the sea, we were left sitting in the sun on the sand, beside the old conch-shell the fishermen used to summon villagers for their catch, and summon villagers to a death by drowning, of a fisherman. The sun was going down now, far out behind the water, beyond the power of our eyes to focus; and the afternoon was still hot, and the water was washing in, lazily and without the rising waves, and no sand mixed in the waves, washing our bodies up to

2

our waists. The water mixed with the sand had the same consistency as the Cream of Wheat porridge our mothers made us eat for breakfast and for strength, to make us men. The conch-shell did not move, or lean over from its majesty, from the touch of the waves.

Our bathing pants, as we called them, were made of khaki. They had tabs, and five buttons to protect our small parts and keep our manhood private. They were the same pants we had worn to high school, when they were new. Now, they were tattered. They were torn in many places, always in the shape of an L. They were cut down, and they reached almost to the knee. We did not wear the leather belts through the tabs as we did when they formed part of our school uniform. And now that they were being soaked in the salt blue waves, they became heavy and were sticking to our bodies, like a second skin.

John was showing me again how double-jointed he was, and was walking on his hands, with legs buckled back. He looked like a crab. He was laughing as he walked on his hands, and I was laughing too. He was laughing as he walked too close to the water, into a wave which threw him into the sea. He lost his balance. And then he screamed. He had stepped on a cobbler. The cobbler, from its colour, which is black, is the dangerous cousin of a sea-egg, which we ate, and which is pink and very delicious, like the meat of conchs. The cobbler, John said, was angry with him. John was reading books about the mysteries of the East. The cobbler broke off about ten short and ugly needles into his foot. The ten needles were visible. Black against the rich pink of his heel. The needles were circled by ten spots of blood. Just the tops. I could see them clearly against the dark, fat pink of his sole near the heel. All ten were in the heel of his left foot.

He had just told me that he was double-jointed, like an Indian swami. He had shown me how double-jointed he was. The evening before, while sitting on the sand, he had grabbed his right leg with his right hand, and put it over his head. I had closed my eyes, expecting to hear his joints break. But nothing happened. All I could hear when he did this trick was the lapping of water against the pink shell of the conch. He looked like the old man who walked on the seat of his pants, with his hands moving his crippled body, propelled inch by inch, over the hard concrete pavement of the main street in Town, where he begged for pennies, looking up at the towering passengers in the buses which looked like the buildings he had stormed in France when he fought in a war that ended before the Second World War began, when he lost his legs, when he could walk, when he stepped on a mine.

When John did the same trick with his left leg, I closed my eyes again. And when I opened them, I thought John had turned into a large soldier-crab. All I could hear was the water running back into the sea, passing over the stationary conch-shell, laughing and ignoring the inability of the shell to follow it back into the deep. His joints did not break. He believed in the mysteries of the East. I knew then that he was double-jointed. And I told him that his joints were made of rubber.

"Rubber?" he asked me. "Like the rubber in our inner tube?"

"Indian rubber," I said.

Our inner tube, patched in many different colours of rubber, black, brown, and red, was just then drifting out to sea. The tide had come in while I was watching John's transformation into a soldier-crab, and a wave falling back upon itself had dragged it, like a thief, out of our reach. Stealthily, the wave took the inner tube on which we would sit in the lolling sea, like it would take a crab, transparent through to its stomach, who scampers up the beach, grabs its prey, and disappears into the retreating waves that hide the prey and the crab because they have the same colour as the preda-tory crab. The waves were filled with these killing crabs. John was able to swim. But the ten black points circled and highlighted by the ten spots of blood in his pink heel were stinging him. He had washed his heel in the salt water twice, but with no relief.

John could do almost everything better than me, better than any boy in the neighbourhood could do, or was supposed to do: playing cricket, football, running to victory as the young champion athlete, playing tennis in the road with wooden rackets he made him-self, fishing for sprats, coming first in class, and talking to three girls at the same time and making each of them his confidante. And he was head boy and soloist in the choir of St. Matthias Anglican Church. John was the star. The ten cobblers were still stinging his foot. He had promised many times to teach me how to swim, but he always forgot. He made this promise every long vacation, but he never remembered. And anyway, the sea at this time of year was often rough, with the winds of hurricanes and storms.

"The tube! The tube! Man, look the inner tube!"

And I got up from the sand, which had caused my bathing pants to be wet in the entire seat, and I ran towards the water. And stopped dead. And I thought of the waves coming up to my shoulders, and then to my neck, and then to my head, and then into my mouth. And I saw again, as if it was happening in front of me, as I faced the waves, my uncle's bloated body, filled with sea water and with some sprigs of moss that had got into his mouth, heavy and dead, while the other fishermen were dragging him in the same way they had earlier dragged the two-ton body of a shark over the beach, out of the water, along the sand, and the dragging of my uncle was the leaving of the trail of his limp body and legs over the sand, scratching it in two places like the lines of a railway track, the evidence of the passage of body and legs over the sand that remained the colour of the shell of the conch, the marking-out of his last journey from the sea. When the shark was dragged in triumph over the pink sand, the mark it left was the one thick imprint of its tail. We ate the shark afterwards, in two hours, in vengeance, fried or boiled in steaks thick as our hands. And we ate it with the same glee as my uncle had told me sharks ate men, including fishermen. That Sunday afternoon, after church and Sunday school, when my uncle was returned home, as large as a buffalo with the water in his body and his lungs, someone blew the conch-shell, too. It was a man. He tried his hand and his talent at a hymn from the book of *Hymns Ancient & Modern*, something fitting for a fisherman, something fitting for a man whose life was lost at sea. The man tried his own lungs against the pink coral makeshift instrument of the conch, and made the village sadder with a mournful rendition of the hymn sung in the Litany for those in peril on the sea. Hymn 624. John and I knew the hymn. It was sung every morning for the whole week at school, Monday, Tuesday, Wednesday (which was the day we ate shark soup for lunch), Thursday, and Friday, (which was choir practice at St. Matthias Anglican Church, fifty yards from our homes); and we sang it too, in memory and in honour of uncles, brothers, and fathers who had tried their luck with employment, by fighting on the side of the "Allieds" in the Second World War. We sang that hymn more often than we sang "Evening Shadows Make Me Blue," sang it so often that John and I knew it by heart, although we could never find it in the hymn-book, unless the Headmaster had first told us the number and the page. But that Sunday afternoon, the man blew the conch-shell, without benefit of music lessons and the right key, and we still were able to recognize that it was the hymn for those in peril on the sea.

"The blasted tube, man!" John reminded me. "The tube!" John was hopping on one leg, waving his hands and pointing to the black inner tube of the car tire which was our lifeguard. "Swim, man! Swim-out and save the blasted tube!"

I remembered the "moses," the small boat my uncle used to shuttle and push himself over the soft, placid water near the shore, level as glass, and how he guided himself in this small boat with one oar into the deeper water, to reach his fishing boat. His fishing boat was tied with a thick piece of rope that he made stronger by rubbing it with some something the local joiner and cabinet-maker had given him; and tied at the sunken end of the rope, far far down into the sea you could not see from the surface, was a piece of concrete, heavy as iron, which he called his anchor. I remembered how he would hop into the "moses" as if he were hopping onto a passenger bus to escape paying the fare, and before I could blink my eyes twice, in the twinkling of an eye, "before you could say Jack-Sprat!" as my mother always said about his shuttling from the land to the deep sea in the fragile "moses," before I could twink an eye, he would disappear amongst the climbing waves, higher than the steeple of the church, higher than any hill in Barbados, and then I would hold my breath; and when I released it, the "moses" would be like a hat thrown into the sea, or a leaf, dancing in a frolic upon the steadying waves. "The sea is a bitch!" he would say, when he emerged from the glistening, shiny, silver waves, after having toiled all night in the thick, oily blackness out of sight of land. He would come back with only one cavalley, one barracuda, and six flying fish as his reward, flat and squiggling on the bottom of the large boat made with his own hands. "A bitch, boy!" But it was enough. Enough to feed even his family, not counting the three outside-children that he had, and a few women on the side. Friends and lovers in equal proportion of commitment and pleasure always shared his catch. "This sea," he would say, pointing back to the vast beautiful water which the early evening sun had made glorious, "*That* sea? Is a bitch!" Then, at last, before my loss of breath and patience, he would reach the fishing boat, which he had christened *Galilee* with a bottle of white rum that contained only one gill. He had drunk the rest before the ceremony. He was a deacon in the Church of the Nazarene, when he was not catching jacks and sprats, flying fish and sharks, dolphins and conger eels, and other "breeds," as he called them. He didn't go to church too often; but he never ventured into the sea on Sundays to fish, except early Sunday morning, just a few hundred feet from the shore, to fetch-back the fish-pots from the rewarding sea, pots filled with after-morning-church dinner of barbaras, cavalleys, ning-nings, sea-eggs when they were in season, and when it was still illegal to catch them during those months whose names did not end in "er."

But the last syllable in the name, the "er," was always disregarded by him. And once, to our religious joy, one bright Sunday morning, the fish-pots blessed us with a lobster. It weighed twenty pounds, one ounce.

"Jesus Christ!" the other fishermen and two women sitting on the sand with baskets and buckets screamed.

"A twenty-pung, one-ounce lobster, man?" my aunt had said, hefting the thing in her left hand, and with a stick in her right, ready to strike it dead if it wriggled the scissors of its big and little claws too close to her face. "Man, whoever hear of a lobster this size, that weigh twenty pungs, one ounce? You not 'fraid God strike you dead? And on a Sunday morning, to-boot?"

"Well, not that in the real sense I mean that this lobster which I catch tip the scales at twenty pungs avoirdupois, plus one ounce," he said, respectful, though relishing his use of big words, which he loved as much as he loved his sister. But he had no scales. He never relied on them, but weighed everything, fish, potatoes, and mangoes, by hand, hefting them. "When I say that she tipping the scales at twenty pungs, one ounce, assuming that I did-have a blasted pair o' scales, is only a way o' speaking, girl. Only a way o' speaking!"

It was just two weeks after that Sunday morning that they brought him back, as if he were a shark he himself had caught, out in the darkness, putting an end to his fishing on the Sabbath, as he called Sundays, although he did not know what the difference meant.

"Swim-out! Swim-out!"

10

John's voice, meanwhile, is ringing in my ears, but I am seeing the "moses" drifting in the trough of waves; then *Galilee*, then the darkness; then the blowing of the conch-shell horn that killed the smaller signals from the doves-of-the-woods; and then the bruised sand over which they are dragging my uncle's body, bloated by water, bloated with more water than my teacher in elementary school had told me was the correct proportion for a human carcass; and then the darkness.

"Swim-out! Swim-out!"

I stood my ground. I saw the black tube do the same dance as the "moses" used to do. I saw it disappear. I saw it reappear. I saw it get small and smaller, smaller still, until it was the same size, the same black mark, as one of the ten needles of the cobbler in the pink skin of John's heel. That was the last time I saw the tube. That was the last time I ever sat on the sand with John. That was the last time, before I left the island, with John following soon behind, when we did almost everything together or had it done to us: birth, baptism, christening, and confirmation; leaving elementary school for the Combermere School for Boys where they trained us boys and turned us into senior civil servants and junior civil servants too; times when we joined the choir of St. Michael's Cathedral Church, after St. Matthias, where we learned to memorize Roman numerals before we could follow the announcement of Psalms at matins and at evensong, and then find them in the red leather-bound Psalter; times in Scouts, cadets, Harrison College, a first-rate school for boys also, and only, and for turning us into barristers-at-law, and doctors, and priests to replenish the Anglican church, and secondary school teachers at our old school and college; for early, forced marriedhood, if girl friends were made pregnant by an error of youth and passion; and for university. Canada for me, because my money was too short to stretch across the Atlantic Ocean on a boat and go to Oxford; and Amurca for John, because his ship-working uncle was now docked and hiding in Brooklyn, for ten years, among the waves of other daring, risk-taking men, and was safe between the waves of the Stars and Stripes . . .

I am walking in the snow now. The snow is deep. And my legs are heavy from pushing aside the tiring snow, which the plough that passes beside me is barely able to do; and I feel I am walking in frozen water. I have not remembered to take my shoes to the shoemaker to cover the hole in the middle of the left sole. So many things that I plan to do, late at night, and the night before, and put them down in diaries, and I forget them all, in this clenching and undying snow and cold, when morning comes. And I am slipping. I am moving one heavy foot no match for the cold leaking through my left sole; moving one foot at a time, at the same pace as the old blackened sail I used to see far out at sea, on that same beach where we sat, John and I, forty-fifty years ago, counting the steamers and the Canadian lady-boats and inter-island schooners which brought strangers and thieves, whose language was French and broken English, and "pahwee-mangoes" and bananas and nutmegs, weaving through the string of pearls and water surrounding us, to our shore. It is about eleven o'clock now, a time when there would be sun above my head; but here there is no sun overhead, and today, in December, almost noon, it feels as if it is night. Time in this city has made this walking sail old and worn and tattered, so that when the wind is cold and strong as it is today, holes in the sail you can put your fist through appear; and the wind can go through them, and delay the motion and the speed of arrival. But I am going nowhere in particular. I have no destination. I have no hour of an appointment; for the sail that gives me movement is patched with the words of an old song, in the voice of a woman. I can hear her voice now, whenever I walk these streets in winter . . . walking and seeing a light shining. When I walk there is no light. I can't even remember the words . . . something about being released, being released any day. Any day now, I hope to be released from this snow. I walk and people are passing me by, and I say hello, as I have been taught to do, back in the island, but still I can see nobody waving back hello, for my eyes can only look at you . . . Lang . . . It is not an ordinary face that I look out for, as I walk these streets.

This snow I am walking in now is anticipated and wished for with fierce resolution every December, just before Christmas, when I wish and pray and plan and curse and vow that this Christmas will be the very last, when I dream it is going to be my last. And I have conversations of reproof with myself, for having remained amongst its whiteness for so long, so many winters, all these forty or fifty years; and still I find myself today, this afternoon in December 1996, walking in the same snow, on the same lonely street which remains clean for the short lifetime of its whiteness, a second after the snow hits the pavement.

I say to myself on the twenty-sixth of December every year, as I have been saying for forty-fifty years, "I am going back home, I am going back home, I am going back home," recalling the three times written in a legal warning.

And then myself says to me, "You're damn right! You should haul your arse outta this damn country. What has this goddamn country given you? With all the richness and racism building up, year by year?"

And I argue back with myself, "I have a house. Don't have to rent from no blasted landlord. I have no children. Never had a wife: but a good woman, one short time, filled with flowers and summer; and she died too soon, and she ain't here, no more! Made a living. Making a living . . ."

And myself would argue back, "On that Rock where you born, boy! On that Rock, you can walk down the road, any road, without anybody looking at you the wrong way, and smile and say hello, and hear the greeting coming back, 'cause home is home."

And I would have the final word in this interminable two-timing monologue, forty-fifty years long. "Who do I know still, back home? They're all dead. Or gone-away. Living in Britain; one in Germany as I read in a foreign newspaper; a few in Italy; thousands in Amurca; and tens of thousands unknown to the Immigration authorities, also living in Brooklyn. I do not see them; I see their cousins every year here, in the last week in July and the first week in August; here in Toronto, with their strange, loud, over-sized clothes and thin shins; and gold round their necks, their wrists, their ankles, forgetting the first enchainment in ships; and now they come with gold on all ten fingers sometimes, beating the authorities and the rate of exchange, and in enough quantity and shininess to fill many tombs in Egypt that used to be inhabited by Pharaohs, but not all of the same quality.

Each December, the snow becomes thicker and my resolution thinner, and more difficult to walk on; and it seems to stick to my body like old white paint, except that it has more weight than paint; and I move just like *Galilee*, that overladen fishing boat we used to watch far out in the waves which made it behave as if it was sliding between hills and valleys. John and I spent hours and hours on the warm sand of that beach the colour of the old conch-shell, looking out at those waves, wondering where they went to after they were born at our feet, after they left us, and left our eyesight; wondering how many ships, steamers, Canadian lady-boats, inter-island schooners, and brave fishing boats had passed over those same waves; wondering which wave would bear a woman in its hold that we would truly love, and which ship would carry us from our governors and pageantry and fun and parades and colonialism.

"We's colonials," John said. "And as colonials, we have to leave this place."

"And go where? Where to?" I asked.

"*Anywhere.*"

"We are not really colonials, are we? This is our home. We born here. And after Cawmere School, and Harsun College, we'd be *fixed*. For life."

"The meaning of a' island," John said, "is that you have to swim-out from it, seeing as how it is surrounded by water. And anything surrounded by water is a place you really don't know the size of, like you have to swim-way far from it, and then you would know the measurements of the place. That is the meaning of borning in a' island. There is a book in the Public Library that I was reading; and what I just tell you I was reading is in that book."

"What it name?" I asked John, who was always reading in "reading-races" with me, with books we borrowed every Saturday morning from the Library in Town. "What is the name of that book?"

"Man, I read it in a book, man," he said, "and if I read it in a book, it is true. So I don't have to tell you *nothing* more! The only important thing for you to know is that it is printed in a book. Books don't lie."

"But you really thinking of not living in this place?"

"The minute I finish school, out-goes-me! I gone!"

"To where?"

"Brooklyn, New York, with my uncle. Europe. Any place. But I know I will not be living in this place."

"Me, too," I said. And it scared me because I did not know where I could go; and it scared John that I was thinking along the same lines.

Of course, we did not live through those times knowing it was anything like colonialism. We watched the Governor drive through our neighbourhoods, in his black, polished Humber Hawk, on his way to parades; and going to friends to drink rum and soda, and gamble with cards; and when his car stopped within touching distance, we stared at its glamour, and saw our faces in the sparkling bonnet. And once we caught him at a hotel, the Colony Club, where men who governed the island, although they were not governors, but only played polo, and drank whisky and soda, and lived in large houses, met to drink after a game; and we saw our faces again, and our grinning teeth in the bonnet of the glimmering Humber Hawk, while the chauffeur, a man elevated from our village, and dressed like an officer in evening uniform of black, deep black, stood beside the car, rubbing it down with a yellow chamois cloth, as if he was rubbing down a woman's thighs, as if he had not rubbed it down for hours, one hour before he left the Governor's House, making it shine, from any distance, like a dog's stones on a dark night.

"You two sons o' bitches, *no more further*! You hear me? Do *not* touch the kiss-me-arse white man's moto-car! You hear me?"

John and I did not really live under the yoke of colonialism, as we had read in our library books that Africans did still. We said we were colonials because we were joking; because it was just our young fury and our imitating the words of older men and the book-learning we were getting at Combermere School for Boys that made us see ourselves as colonials, sitting on that sand on that beach, staring at waves that washed assertive and sullen strangers ashore, as if they were born like us, in the island, as if they were born here, to rule over us, here. We knew only what it could mean to be sitting on the sand all day, every day; and dreaming; and pretending we were the brother of that little boy who, in the poem we had to learn by heart, stood in his shoes and wondered, he stood in his shoes and he wondered; and we wondered why. We did not remember the name of the book or the poem in which we had read about this little boy and liked him. We did not wear shoes while we wondered whether the wave that licked our feet and our pink heels, the wave that brought the fateful cobbler into John's pink heel, that washed my uncle in, dead and swollen, was the same wave born in another country, and that had travelled alongside the steamer and the Canadian lady-boats and deposited the little blackened piece of wood, or stick, or flotsam and jetsam, at our feet. Or whether it was the same wave as those thousands which washed the ships of groaning Africans sardined in holds on our beaches where the tourist hotels are built. In my elementary school, Mr. Thorpe, our teacher, stood one afternoon before our class, First Standard, with sweat of his honest underpaid labour pouring off his face, as the tears poured from our eyes, as he poured "comma-sense" into our heads and ears and backs and backsides, because we had not remembered that a little piece of blackened stick, or wood, was properly known as "flotsam." He screamed as he poured the knowledge into our small minds and bodies.

"*Flotsam!* The proper word is *flotsam*! What is the proper word? Say it again! Flot-*sam*! *Flot*-sam!" And each stress of pronunciation was riveted home with the heavy hand of pronouncement from the pronunciating tamarind rod. The rod of tearful justice. And from that soaked afternoon, I associated the two words to have the same meaning: *pronunciation* and *pronouncement*. But we were acquainted with another kind of "flotsam," since one or two of us, not John and I, were sometimes called "the flotsam of our society." It was the English vicar, one morning at matins, from the pulpit made of lignum vitae by the hands of the village's cabinet-makers, who polished wood to make it look like brass, it was the Vicar who used the word which almost slipped by us, as it was spoken in his *accent* which we could hardly understand, but which we killed ourselves afterwards imitating. "*Flott-sum!*" And after that sermon, we too called those other little boys by this name. But we thought of ourselves as *that* other little boy in the poem about boys wearing shoes, standing and wondering.

It is about, it is, I think, a little after eleven o'clock on this cold day in December; and I am walking north along Yonge Street, just up from a place which used to be a commercial bank and which now looks like an abandoned church; and bag men and homeless women have made it their drinking place where they sleep on sheets of thin cardboard, making it look like an institution for justice and a prison in Latin America; and up from this camping ground are the stores open today by Indian immigrants from Sri Lanka and Pakistan and Trinidad, and closed tomorrow by the Housing Authorities sent by the police, for reasons the Sri Lankans cannot interpret; up from the southernmost end of the Eaton Centre, across the street; up from Massey Hall off that short street, walking in a kind of white valley, for the thickness of the snow has hidden all these buildings from easy sight, and I can only know they are there from memory. And the snow has hidden all colour and life from the street, and the Christmas colours of green and red, silver and gold, from store windows; and I am alone, and I can see nobody, and nobody can see me. There are only shapes; the shapes of people I hear ahead of me. I raise my head against the flakes that enter my eyes, almost blinding me, and those that fall into my ears, tickling me; and I try to laugh at this short tickle, to see the fun in it; but there is no sky, and no sun, and no warm sand, only a channel of white. I am walking through a valley with no landmarks on my left side, or my right, to give me bearing and remind me of the notice of movement, although I know I am travelling forward, north, since I have set out from the bottom of the street, by the Lake.

It is only in the past five years, after my forty-fifty years of complaining about winter, and my threats to myself about going back home, that I find myself walking beside the Lake, wondering what would happen. The Lake is a lake. It is not the sea. There are seagulls but no scratching crabs; and the boats are larger and from larger countries; and no sand on the shore, there is no beach; and no waves; but it is the closest thing I can come to, in the absence of sand of any colour, like the conch-shell on that beach. The Lake is a place I can sit beside and dream of waves and the origin of waves and where waves can take you. I stand leaning on the metal rail guarding the Lake, preventing my jump, in this tormenting time of indecision: home or here; sun or snow; and I have thought, many times, that at this age, and with the leisure that age brings and that hangs languorously on my hands, of attempting precisely that. Jumping into the Lake. "Jump in the goddamn Lake, you bugger!" a man told me, forty years ago. I was working in the summer in a Flo-Glaze factory as a part-time worker, a working man, when I was a student at Trinity College; and I had put the wrong measurement of percentages and paints and concentrated tints in the order I was given to fill. "Go jump in the fucking Lake!" This was the advice a woman gave when I could not fill the order of her love, when she said she knew that she loved me, after I had asked her to marry me. I was a student out of work, then. Jumping into the Lake. I have tried it often in my mind, but the metal rail prevents me.

On that afternoon back in the island, with sun and light and sky blue as the desire for Chermadene, a young schoolgirl who John and I, as in many things, liked with the same passion, we did not talk about lakes. But we talked about Chermadene. John and I fell in love with this girl with the plaited hair. And she always wore two dangling blue pieces of ribbon in her hair. On that warm afternoon, on the beach, when the needles of the cobbler were in John's heel, we still talked and argued about her. And our words of little competition had prevented us from seeing the inner tube float out into the deeper water; and we could not retrieve it, this black, patched tube that we had got from a tire off the Humber Hawk. The tire was no longer roaring and screeching along the narrow crowded streets of our neighbourhood. Once, before we got it, it was killing not only two chickens that laid one egg a day, but one man who was out of work, and who moved too slowly out of the road. On that afternoon, I wished the tire would develop a leak and sink with me on it, and end the pain of Chermadene's divided love. But when on that afternoon on the beach we looked up to see the tube, a million times larger than the Lifesavers which the tourisses brought into the island and which we sucked in slow delight, I was rendered then as unmovable as the Humber Hawk has become. For it was now placed on four large coral stone blocks, to be scavenged by the apprenticed mechanics in the village. On that afternoon, I could not retrieve the life-saving tube, as I could not make it sink, and would be drowned. Because I could not swim.

And I know now, though at that time on the beach I was too young to possess this heavy knowledge about suicide, that only those who swim can attempt to jump into a lake, to put an end to their lives and to their loves. Money. Love. The lack of money. The loss of love. Those of us who cannot swim are too particular about drowning to test the consolation of the water.

Money and love flow past us, like the waves on that beach with that inner tube that drowned at sea; or was lost. And no man came to put the voiceless conch-shell to his lips.

So, when I ducked my head to shake the snow from out of my ears, I became unbalanced, and I almost got knocked down by the shape coming invisible and silent through the thick mist of snow. He did not see me. She did not see me. I try to be fair in this city, where I cannot be as sure as an oath taken upon the thin page of the Holy Bible, that I can say with truth and sureness, that it is a man or a woman coming against me, that it *is* a man; or if I say it is a woman coming against me, that *she* is a woman. Men and women in this democratic, fun-loving, gay city, coated at this time of year in deep, falling snow and wool, all look the same. Sometimes the bodies of men and women shake and behave the same.

The shape did not see me. I was just another obstacle that the shape had to walk around, or walk into, continuing in its journey, with spirited childlike glee at the fresh fall of this thickness that transformed the sidewalk into a skating rink.

This snow, through which I am trying to move, and which I am trying to like, as if I were born to its thickness and trickiness underfoot, and in which I live, is a curtain. It reminds me of the thick white ones, *sheers*, which my mother strung with herringbone twine, at each of the sixteen windows in our walled house, a house with six gables or roofs. These curtains looked and behaved like six waves or big sails against the wind and the blue sea, if you were sitting on the sand and watching them.

And I can see nothing in front of me now. Nothing. But I try to pretend that I am native to this kind of treachery on ice, that I was born here into this white, cold miserableness, and am not really an obstacle.

A new spasm of life comes into my steps. My feet become less heavy. I am back there. And the wet khaki cut-down pants have dried suddenly in the sun; and I am a sprinter running through thick green fields of sugar cane and cush-cush grass after the animals, my mother's livestock, goats and sheep and pigs and pigeons. And I hear a voice. Her voice? The chauffeur's voice? Coming out of this thick snow which blindfolds the afternoon. Out of this surrounding curtain comes a voice. "Move-out o' my goddamn way, man!" The words injure the sweet, white silence of the snow. "What the arse . . . ?"

It is like a voice crying out from amongst thick belching smoke and crackling shingles, of a house on fire, burning for help and assistance. But it is also a voice of anger. I know the anger in the voice of a burning house. I have heard it many times. Voices like this come after a ball bowled too fast and causing injury. This is a voice that comes after a race that is lost, after a wrong key in a solo, in a descant. It is as if the burning house and the white snow engulfing it has to clear before I can learn the distinctness in the voice. The second reprimand is a longer declaration for assistance. This makes the thick smoke clear. It is a voice I know. I heard it once on a beach. "What the arse . . . You want to lick me down, man?"

Still, I cannot see. No shape, or owner of this voice. And in this blinding snow he cannot see me. But I stop walking, though I am unable to stand motionless, in this snow which shifts like an uncontrollable roller skate, for too long. My shoes are sliding. I can feel winter on my soles. My left foot is wet from the soaked, cold, woollen sock. And I go back to that time, on a pasture, the Garrison Savannah Parade Ground, so hot and so sticking wet, when I was made to stand at attention, while the Governor moved through our ranks taking his royal time, and I could barely see him in the distance; for in that regal distance, the Governor was nothing more than a bunch of regimental plumes, all white. At that distance, it was as if he were a gigantic common fowl-cock or a Leghorn about to crow the morning in, from the top of the wooden fence, his roost surrounding our yard, and bring his hundred hens to sexual attention. This voice, though, is the same voice I had heard next to me, as I wavered while ordered to stand at "atten-shunn!"; when the water in my bladder was making it impossible for me to be rigid and soldierly, when I moved ever so slightly to ease the pain and the burning of the sun and the sweat pouring down my face and into my neck, making the khaki uniform shirt no longer stiff, and down into the white, blancoed belt me and my mother had laboured over, and changed from green canvas to spotless white.

I am now close enough to stand, to see. And to wonder. And recognize. And call back, in this thickening snow, in this flash of abusive time, all those years.

"John!"

"You?"

"*John?*"

"Goddamn, man!" he says. I am sitting beside him once more, on the warm afternoon sand. And an inner tube is drifting out, into the sea, into the Atlantic which we knew would join us up again, some time later, in a land too far for our young eyes to see, after it has separated us.

"Jesus Christ!" I say, giving the miracle of this reacquaintance credence and reality, giving the sudden reunion its greeting of incredulity, giving his appearance its dramatic significance.

"*You?*" he asks, believing and not believing.

How can he believe so easily, in this mist of time, in this street, in this city, in this country which we had not only studied in our geography books at Combermere School for Boys and knew by heart, but still had refused to believe to be the place we would choose to live in? In this North America? In all these forty-fifty years we had not once exchanged even a post card at Christmas. Birthdays were forgotten landmarks. And the telephone neither of us thought about. It was out of the question.

In all this time, neither of us knew we would voluntarily live with this cold, this ice, this snow.

"God bless my eyesight!" I say.

"Too goddamn good to be true!" he says.

"Jesus Christ!"

"If anybody had-tell me that you and me, who last see each other sitting-down that afternoon on the beach by Paynes Bay! Look at this thing, though! God bless *my* eyesight! How long you in this place?"

"This is really you?"

"Is *me*, man!"

"But, Jesus Christ! Not calling the name of the Lord in vain, but this is a goddamn . . . Tell me something, though. I been thinking of this for donkey-years. Must be over forty years now, I been thinking of finding you, to axe you this question. You learn how to swim yet?"

And our laughter explodes. Out of the white mist come shapes which pause to look, to understand, to wonder why this loud tropical laughter and equatorial joy must take place in this deadening cold, to break the quiet peace of this cold, clean afternoon. What could cause this joy? And cause these two old black men to embrace each other, laughing and slipping on the ice, and pummelling each other on the backs of their thick black and light-brown cashmere winter coats, with hands that are magnified in brown leather gloves, weighing down their hands and their bodies bloated by thick scarves and wool and sweaters? I sometimes laugh at myself, as I see my reflection in a store window, as I pass wearing all this clothing, making me walk after all these years with added weight and meaning and cold experience in this new environment, I see how it makes us, at our age, walk with a limp, like huge tamed monkeys, since neither of us has got accustomed to this way of dressing, nor has learned to walk in winter. And all this laughing in the people's street?

We are hugging each other. I am slapping him, he is slapping me on the back, and I am judging how much size he has put on his frail boyhood body. He is slapping me as if he is a Black Muslim. His after-shave lotion is pungent in my nostrils, as he is moving from cheek to cheek slapping me all the time on the back as if he is trying to make me burp, as our mothers used to do after the bottle; and later, after the Cream of Wheat. His after-shave lotion follows me, as he is changing from the left shoulder to the right, when that first shoulder blade has suffered sufficient pummelling from the affection that had first poured on that sand the colour of coral, the colour of the empty conch-shell, when he showed me how to walk on his hands like a crab.

"I *don't* believe my two goddamn eyes!"

"If you want to know the truth," I say, "if you want to know the truth, I was thinking about home, just before I bounced into you."

"Bounce into me? Man, you nearly licked-me-to-fuck down! Goddamn! And a black man like me don't look too good sprawl-out on the goddamn snow! Never learned how to walk in all this goddamn snow in the goddamn winter, after all these years. And never want to, neither!" We stand and stare at each other; and do not talk for a long while; and then the need for time and place and history comes spewing out. "Been in England for years. The Mother Country, eh? Tried Europe for a piece. France and Italy and Germany. Like their food and their women, but not their goddamn language! Catch their winters in my arse! And you know how racist the fuckers are! I hear Canada better. *Liberté* and *égalité*. But France? Those two words are mother-fuckers! Never could figure out how Amurcans like Wright, Richard Wright, and Baldwin could say that France is such a liberal place. France? I had a French wife once. But I never learned to speak their *parlez-vous*. Not one goddamn vowel in *français* pass my lips. Stayed pure-fucking-Barbadian, and spoke the Bajan language. Bajan is *my* foreign language. I spoke it in France as if it was a foreign language. And the French woman that I married would nod her head and say, *oui, oui, oui-oui!* Goddamn! But you was about to say something when I cut-you-off. What was you about to say when I butt-in?"

"I was about to ask you what you're doing here. If you have a family. You're here on a job? A conference? Business . . . ?"

"Man, look at you, though! Look at little Timmy! And not one goddamn grey hair in your head! Still *fooping*? Screwing chicks? You're too goddamn old to be still fooping!" His sudden outburst, like thunder, frightens and embarrasses me. "If you see what I'm saying . . ."

He hollers so much, and so loudly when he says this, and with such wicked warmth, that all those years are peeled back, revealing us and a time when we were in love with the same girl, Chermadene.

"And neither of us really got to first base with her," he says, "because she was a virgin, and because we never played baseball in the island, and because her mother threatened us."

And in his words, I am facing the hurtful memory of those glorious, happy days.

I am standing now in front of a window with men's suits the size of giants, with matching shoes, and the trunks of men with pink skin made of shining plastic, with false silk hair; and I can see rows of shoes of shiny leather and stiff lasts of large feet attached to long trousers, to bodies that end at the waist, as if a mass-murderer has hacked the bodies into halves, and left them in these show windows which look like glass coffins that cannot hold them from head to foot. And my glance touches matching shirts for men made famous in movies about men who like to chop down trees tall as skyscrapers, and have a preference for heights; and I can see the sidewalk now, for to my right are long windows that reach to the ground, all glass with shirts in them, made in foreign countries like the ones John says he lived in, and made by foreign hands, Polo, Yves Saint Laurent, Ralph Lauren, and other designers; and briefcases and travel bags made from the sides of animals which the television says are killed illegally. I can see now where I am standing, and where I am going. I am standing across the street from the south end of the Eaton Centre. It has taken me all this time, in physical movement and in the span of years, to travel this short distance from the edge of the Lake, which before this moment was completely blotted out by the thick falling snow. Now I can see where I am standing and where I am going. It is as if John's breath, and the violence he has put into his laughing speech, his exuberance and warmth, show me how unsmiling an old man's walk, this afternoon in December, has been.

The snow has disappeared. All around us, it seems, the street and the sidewalk have come alive. And I am sure also that we two black men, old geezers as they call us in this city, and as we appear, two old-age pensioners, we two old West Indian men are the only two living, happy persons in the world, on this cold honest Toronto afternoon. It is like sitting on that warm sand, possessing the entire beach and owning our lives, conquerors of the entire beach, and with no one in sight, no one threatening, no one pretending to our throne of ownership.

"Where's the nearest bar? This calls for a drink. Goddamn!" John says.

"Not a drink, man. *Drinks!*" I say.

"Do you have time? You're on your lunchtime?" he says.

"I don't work," I tell him.

"Unemploy, huh? Goddamn!"

"I don't work."

"Goddamn! You're retired, then?"

"I am not retired."

"Goddamn! Things tough with everybody these days? But you still hustling the chicks, though!"

"I am free. Of chicks and work. The only work I do is walking. I walk all day. Work is for immigrants. I was never an immigrant. Ten years ago I stopped working. Nowadays I just walk. As the song says, *I walk the lonely streets*. Ten years almost to the day . . . the twenty-six of this month is . . ."

"You won't be pimping, would ya?"

"Just walking. And looking at people, and . . ."

"If a man don't work, he's gotta be pimping. And I don't mean *you* personally, nor that you be pimping off chicks, if you see what I mean."

". . . but the twenty-six of this month ten years ago is when I made up my mind not to lift another finger even if it was to save my life. Not since eighty-six, or eighty-seven. December the twenty-six, nineteen hundred and eighty-seven, to be exact. I have it written down. I even walk with it in my wallet. Been doing that for years! Right here. When we sit down, I'll show you the note, the reminder I wrote to myself, December the twenty-six, nineteen eighty-seven."

"Goddamn!"

We are walking slowly now. We are looking for the nearest bar. The snow is deep, and fresh and beautiful like clouds you see from the windows of planes travelling to the West Indies. The snow is pure and enervating as a morning sea bath, when you enter the water first, and here no human foot has touched the long unsullied stretch ahead of us. Our footsteps are slipping still, from the hidden ice. But we are in no hurry to get anywhere.

John's hand is on my shoulder as we walk, as we used to stand on the school pasture talking, at lunch and after school, while he prepared to take batting practice in the nets: he to bat, and I to watch. "You shoulda seen the length of those needles from the cobbler that came outta my foot that night! One inch long, at least, every one o' them. But, getting back to you . . ."

"Here we are!" I say, and we enter the bar we are standing beside.

The bar is almost empty. We move to the rear, in the semi-darkness, away from the entrance, from the sudden blasts of cold, and to give rein and space to the explosion of our happiness in our dramatic chance meeting. When we get accustomed to the new, subdued light in the bar, we see two other men, younger than ourselves, sitting at opposite ends of the long bar itself, drinking draught beer. One of them has just said, "Another Bud, eh, Bud?" And the man behind the bar comes out of the darkness, whistling a tune, and nods in our direction.

"In all this time, in all these years, you ever wondered what happen to me, or where I was?" John asks. "I never wrote, not even a card, 'cause I didn't know how to track you down. In all this goddamn time." He slaps me on the back, hard, and says, "I'm here for a few days only. Came in two nights ago."

"Never," I say, about the writing.

"I never wrote you a letter. From all those different foreign countries!" John says. "Knew, though. Knew

I'll bump into you, one o' these days. Here, or back home. Perhaps, on the beach back home."

"Ever thought of going back home?"

"Three times. After each divorce. Three times, but never tried it. Thought of it though," John says, "to relax, and to dead. That's all home means to me!"

"Can't decide myself, either."

"Get married? Ever get married?" John says.

"Going back? I'm not going back, even to die."

"Shit, I can't even ask you what you're drinking these days," John says, "'cause when we last was together, neither you nor me was drinking liquor, To me, though, you look like a Scotch man. Right?"

"Scotch and soda," I tell him. The other man drinking draught raises his hand towards the barman, who says, "Another draught?" And the man says, "Yeah, Bud."

"Goddamn! You know something?" John says. "Something I been watching on television lately, that have to do with twins. Two twins. I never had twin-brothers, as you know. Nor twin-thrildren. I know you don't have twins in your family. But this thing about twins and their habits. Generical twins, they call it. Where one go, the other is sure to go. Goddamn! Just like that nursery rhyme we had to learn by heart in elementary school! *Mary had a little lamb, the lamb was white as snow, and every goddamn way that Mary split to, the goddamn lamb was sure to go!* These generic twins. Where one goes, even in secret, the other twin was sure to go! Who one *foops*, the other one is *sure* to *foop*. Ain't that a motherfucker? Now, I axe you, *how* goddamn would I, even though I am a therapist who haven't seen you in forty-something, fifty-somebody years, how would I *know* that your drink is Scotch, not seeing you after all this goddamn time? Forty years? Or fifty?"

"Forty-fifty," I say. But I am wondering what he means about being a therapist. I do not think of asking him. "Forty-fifty."

"Gotta be *more*."

"Fifty years at least! It was nineteen forty-three. The War was still on. We were ten at the time."

"Goddamn! That makes *you* sixty-three!"

"Makes you, too!"

Another man enters the bar and orders a beer. "Any brand," he says. "Cold today, eh, Buddy?" he adds; and I know now that the barman's name is Buddy. It is warm in this bar, and friendly; and I am thirsty; but John is talking and talking; and Buddy looks at us, wondering. John has just gestured to him, to wait a minute. I can feel the cold thawing from my feet.

"Goddamn! We're pensioners, goddamn!" John says.

"I may be sixty-somebody years," I say, "but I'm no damn pensioner. I will never be a Canadian pensioner! And live in a home for the aged!"

"Goddamn! But you never learn to swim! In all this time. That cobbler," he says, in the way men remember events that have changed a part of their lives, "that cobbler that I stepped on, that day." To me, life is

nothing but a cobbler. We have stepped on cobblers all
our lives, while searching for sea-eggs. But he is bring-
ing it back with his powerful memory of nostalgia; and
he makes the cobblers almost as important as all the
good times we had on that beach, as important as
Chermadene. He does not know this, but his nostalgia
brings back Chermadene, and blue, warm water. "I
never had the chance before this, after all these years,
this late, since you left the island before me, I didn't
have the chance to tell you what happened when I got
home that evening bleeding from a cobbler in my heel,
and had to face my Old Lady, my mother . . ."

"How's the Old Lady?"

"Dead."

"I'm sorry. How long? God rest her soul."

He makes the sign of the Cross on the breast of his
tailored winter coat, before taking it off. The cold has
gone out of his bones, too.

"Long. Died when I was still in France. Got the news
from a cousin, and when the letter came, it was three
weeks old, redirected from a previous address; and the
son of a bitch, you remember him? My third-cousin?"

"Smitty?"

"The son of a bitch didn't learn enough French in
First Form, and still there he was, in Barbados, writing
my address in French! So, you know what happen? If
only the son of a bitch had learn a *little* more French,
the letter woulda arrived in time, *at least* for me to get
there more sooner . . ."

"You missed the funeral."

"The funeral, wake, first anniversary, every-goddamn-thing! Is something I will never forget. And something I'll never let that son of a bitch forget, either!"

"Old Smitty!"

"Son of a bitch, trying to write me in French, when he didn't even learn it in First Form! You remember how me and you had to help Smitty with his French homework?"

"Smitty was good in Maths, though. But wasn't nothing, *rien*, in French."

"The son of a bitch knew the Geometry textbook by heart. But French? And *francais*? Didn't even know how to conjugate *je suis, tu suis, il suis*. Fuck all! Robbed me of the chance and the honour of liffing my Old Lady's head . . ."

"*C'est la vie*," I say.

"*C'est la-fucking-vie!*" John says. And roars with laughter; and immediately, I forget the death of his mother, the Old Lady, and the grief I can see, even now, on his countenance as he relates the tragedy. I am aware that his Amurcan voice is a bit too loud for this quiet bar. One man of three other persons sitting nearby looks around until his eyes catch mine, and he turns his head, leaving me with his unspoken disgust. John's mother liked me as if I were her own son. "So, the evening in question, when I went-home with the cobblers in my foot, the Old Lady puts me to sit down. The cobblers bursting my arse. The blood clotting. Pure pain. And my Old Lady giving me a sermon 'bout little boys who won't stay away from the beach. And then she take off all my clothes. And she put a' old, large saucepan on the fire, in the backyard. You remember the kitchen in the backyard? You remember the big-rocks, the three big-rocks, or stones, that served as the oven? We call it a stove, or a grate. And she puts some fresh mahogany pods in the fire. And I wondering if she going-bathe me in hot water. And the blaze came up just like how the sun comes up sudden-sudden over the hill in Paynes Bay. And she hot the water. And washed my feet. Both feet. Although, as you know, the blasted needles was only in my *left* foot. Both feet she washed, although I told her and she could see from the blood that the ten black things was in only one foot. The *left* foot. And you know something? You want to hear . . . ?"

"Five of the cobbler's needles walked from your left foot, to your right foot!"

"You was always a goddamn comedian! That's what I always liked about you. You're still a comedian, just like you still can't swim!"

"I was only joking."

"You haven't *change*! Still playing Bob Hope," he says, laughing. People entering the bar glance at us. I feel people in the street can hear his voice. The man who was there first raises his eyes and moves his lips. "That's why I had to axe you if you're still screwing chicks. You haven't change, have you? People don't change. *I* haven't changed." He stops talking. He slams his left foot and then his right foot against the thick carpet, loosening the cramp of the cold in his legs. And then he slaps his large hands together, then he continues, "Mothers are motherfuckers! I mean that in the *best* way, if you see what I'm saying. They're something else! So, the Old Lady washes both my two feet, knowing all the time, as I had-tell her, and as she-had-already herself *inspect* my left foot, that the goddamn cobbler wasn't in but only one foot, my left foot. In one foot. And I forget now . . . I forget that I was going to tell you that the minute *ma mère* washed both feet, the left *and* the right, both of my goddamn heels start to hurt like hell, as if the needles from the cobbler, all ten o' them, was in each heel. Ain't that something? Was only years ago, years after that incident, when I was at university, learning to be a therapist, did I understand the logic, and the psychological reason for that transference. You see where I am coming from? So. As I was saying. She bathes both feet. And she dries-off both feet. I am naked as when she *borned* me, all this time. Ten goddamn years old. Sitting in a wooden chair, one o' those chairs we had in the back-room, a kitchen chair. And I am dangling my two feet, and feeling good. 'Cause, after all, this is the Old Lady . . ."

"A *nice* Old Lady. I remember the Old Lady. She still goes to church? I forget she's dead. You said she's dead. A kind woman. And she liked me."

"Like her very-own son. And then she wipes the foot, the left *and* the right, in a bath towel; and dry-it-off, dry-dry-dry as a biscuit. And she goes to the larder. Brings out this candle-grease. Put it in something, over the fire, raging now like the fires o' hell and damnation, and applies the candle-grease to *both* heels to draw out the damn needles from the cobbler. And as you would understand, on the same fire, on the three big rock-stones, was another pot, the buck-pot, with split-peas and rice, and pig tails and tomatoes cook-down-in-it, and another saucepan, a smaller one, with a dolphin head boil-down with more tomatoes, in a butter sauce."

"I can taste it now! Lord, the food we used to eat!"

"Some of the best goddamn food in the whole *whirl*! Better than all this *hot-cuisine* I had in France!"

"That's what I miss about living here."

"Food! Shit, *mon ami*, living in France and Paree all those goddamn years, and hearing the *françaises*-people talk a lotta shit about *hot-cuisine*, and other *parlez-vous* food, man, many's the nights, either at home with friends in, or in public, in a restaurant, you don't know the number of times I had to pull-up my wife straight, and inform her that all this shit about *hot-cuisine*, garlic-and-shit, can't *touch* the type and quality o' food we devoured in Barbados, that place where we was both borned. You're right! About the quality o' food and *édiments* we used to have!"

"Fish-head boiled-down in tomatoes, and a butter-sauce!"

"Well, that was my supper that evening when we left sitting down on the beach, and me with those damn cobbler-needles, or quills in my arse. And as I telling you now. The Old Lady heat-up the candle-grease. She puts it on a saucer. A saucer we had, that my uncle had-send from Amurca, with the Statute of Liberty on it. Something make-outta brass, or copper, or something that look like that kind o' metal. This Statute-o'-Liberty saucer. And she place that hot candle-grease all over my left-foot heel, all over, and . . ."

"The right heel, too!" I say, hoping to cut him short to order a drink.

"You're goddamn right! Just in case, she says. And wrap-it-up in a' old piece o' shirt. And knot-it-up. And then. She gives me a sponge-bath with miraculous-bush leaves boiled in the water. Man, you can imagine how I did-feel. Relaxed. Like a goddamn *king*. Calm. Loved. The Old Lady's favourite son. Although, as you know, she only has *me*. And I didn't even think or remember the tube going out to sea, and disappearing out in the waves. And never coming back. I never even think of the trouble you was facing when you went home and had to explain to your father and your mother why you was late. I leff you in the lurch, that evening. I leff you, my *ace-boon-coon* in the goddamn lurch, I was so happy with the hot candle-grease on my left and right foot, and the bush-bath and the split-peas-and-rice."

"They never asked me about the tube."

"Never?"

"Neither my mother nor my father. And you know my mother, the schoolmistress!"

"And here I am, in all this time, years and years later, worrying my arse over you, that I had-leff you in the goddamn lurch, tube-wise! But that evening when we leff the beach and I had the quills, or the needles from the cobbler in my left foot, and my Old Lady do what I just tell you she did, there I was, waiting to have the split-peas-and-rice with the fish-head sauce, and I was going to refuse to wake up the next morning, whiching was a Saturday, because of the happiness of my state, or in other words, wake up late-late and meet you at the bus stop to go to the Public Library. And *then*. Then was when I really knew that she was not being so kind to me. It was the biggest flogging I ever got from the hands o' my mother. The worst cut-arse! At first, I thought she was joking. You know my Old Lady! But after the first fifteen lashes, I *knew* she was giving me *two* for each of the needles from the cobbler. But when she get-pass twenty-five, I realize that she had in mind to paint my arse, three times for each cobbler needle, or quill. As a warning, she says. 'I always warn you three times, don't I? Three times is enough warning to you! Before I pass judgement!' And *waps*! I stop counting after that. And from that day, whiching was the last time the Old Lady raised a hand to me, I never allowed even a sea-egg, which as you know is a cousin to a cobbler, a member of that species, to pass my two lips.

The goddamn *françaises* eat cobblers as gourmet food. And I never went-back in the sea."

"You never told me this," I say.

"I was too embarrass. To-besides, we were studying hard for the Scholarship, and you and me was planning to leave the island. Plus, we moved from the district. Remember? And another thing. It turned my mind from really learning to speak French. The first time, the very first time in my life, I find myself now, the moment I meet you, using a few French words which unconsciously I must-have-pick-up, in the five years I was living in Paree when I was married to the first-wife. So, getting back to you, and to eating *hot-cuisine.* When I was in France, one afternoon I am taking a stroll along the Shan-deleezays, or whatever you call it, when all of a sudden I see this stall full-up with cobblers. I stand up . . ." He takes his hand from my shoulder, and stands up. At last, he is ready for me to order drinks. But all he does is stand. He is facing me. I feel he is trying to get Buddy's attention. The men in the bar look at him, wondering what he is about to do. I am wondering, too. His arms are akimbo. And before speaking, he roars again. The two women entering, passing hand in hand, pause, look, and go on walking past our table, as if they had come upon a very offensive but short-lived smell. He is about six-foot-six. "*Mon dieu!* I am walking with my wife, my French wife, and Jesus Christ! I almost drop dead at the sight of cobblers in a market in Paree, in France! I tried to explain to her why I won't let another cobbler, which is what they eat *instead* of our sea-eggs, pass my goddamn two lips. The French eat cobblers, man! The French would eat anything, and call it *hot-cuisine*, if you see what I'm saying. They eat anything. Fix it up with lemon juice, garlic, and olive oil, and call it *hot-cuisine*. In the last five years that I was still living in the island, in Barbados with the Old Lady, a sea-egg never passed my goddamn lips, neither. Far less a cobbler. All the time I talking to you, I trying to remember the word that the *françaises* use for cobblers. I heard the name *cipaille* used once. But I not sure. Anyhow. And in the five or six years o' marriage to Hyacinthe, when I was *parlez-vous* to that woman, my wife, she never spoke one goddamn word o' English. But we had two thrildren together. And that shows you that somehow we still *manage* to communicate."

"What about a drink, John?"

"We're old-talking, man! What's the hurry? You got a goddamn job to go to? Wait a minute . . ."

I am lonelier now that I am sitting beside John. His company heightens the loneliness of yesterday. I am stripped of that loneliness now, though, that he is talking, sitting beside me, as we had sat together on the warm, damp, conch-shell-coloured sand.

He goes on talking about his life in many countries I have not seen, speaking with the same broad Barbadian accent he grew up with, although to show me the difference between us, and his greater sophistication than mine, which I feel he has noticed, he laces his speech with words he has remembered from the languages of those countries. I like the way the touch of French falls off his broad lips, hitting my ears thin and delicate as pastry.

He is wearing a tailored suit, and a custom-tailored shirt. His Old Lady made all his shirts on her old treadle Singer sewing machine. The Singer had no electricity to double her production of clothes and her productiveness and lessen the brute force she had to use by working it with her feet. There was no electricity running through the village or the house. But her artistry on the Singer was not great enough for her to try her hand at making a pair of trousers.

The suit he is wearing now is dark grey, with a thin pinstripe. His shirt is white with French cuffs. I can see his initials, *JDN*, embroidered in blue italics on his shirt pocket. In all the years of separation, my imagination had made his taste more American and conspicuous than he now looks, like parts of his conversation and speech; and I would have dressed him in a heavy faked wool suit with large red squares upon the green cloth, and with cufflinks that are square and shiny and that have animals, or birds the shape of eagles, on them. The cufflinks he is wearing now are thin, conservative ovals of pure gold. His dark grey tie is shiny, made of silk, and tied in a knot that is tight and elongated. The last time I saw a tie tied like this was on the reddened neck of the Headmaster of our elementary school, the Headmaster who wore a pure gold ring round *his* knot.

There is a stiffness in the neck of John's collar, and in his cuffs, just like the Headmaster's. And I remember that John's Old Lady used to take in washing from the crowded hotels where the "tourisses," as his mother called them, stayed along the long stretch of the fresh clean pink beach, called the Gold Coast. I would visit John's house on Saturday afternoons after we had returned from the Public Library. Our arms would be laden with books, more numerous than those read by the entire neighbourhood, except the Headmaster who lived nearby. John and I found out the Headmaster cared for his books, which he bought from England, from Foyles Book Stores, Used and Second-hand, by spraying them generously with kerosene oil. He paid for these imported classical texts out of his meagre salary with money orders, and then was forced to protect the wisdom contained in them – Latin texts, Greek texts, and Roman history – by soaking them page by page, and their hard covers, too, in kerosene oil. The same oil from the lamp he used to study with into the early morning when the conch-shell blew and sounded the arrival of some fishing boats. Yes, on those Saturday afternoons when we returned from the Public Library, when John and I were engaged in "reading races," and he beating me in all of them, and I feeling that at any moment he would burst his brains with all the serious knowledge contained in our small books, just as all the neighbours knew that the Headmaster, seeking greater academic status within our midst, would certainly burst *his* brains from all the serious reading he put himself under, under the faint light from the kerosene lamp, reading and reading for his Bachelor of Arts Degree, External, from London University, Part 1, *Honours,* in Classics. He taught us Scripture, World Geography, Reading and Writing and 'Rithmetics, as he prepared for his greater intellectual prowess. Yes, and on those Saturday afternoons, after we had wrapped our borrowed books in brown shop-paper as John's Old Lady ordered us, "to proteck the learning inside them books, boy! To proteck that precious learning in them books!", I would sit in the open door of the back-room and watch her standing at the wooden kitchen table, which was layered with three white sheets, pinned at the four legs of the battered table for smoothness. I would watch her as the sweat poured off her forehead as she moved the heavy, sturdy clothes-iron over the mountain of clothes. She would pass the sizzling iron, after she had first tested it for hotness close to her jaw, over the sheets and pillow-cases and white shirts interminable as the waves coming up onto the beach and going back into the sea which washed the Gold Coast and the tourisses in the hotels. I could see the waves and the beach and the fishermen and the conch-shell from my seat in the door of her back-house. And sometimes, when she was too tired from ironing the hotel's laundry, she would change to the clothes that John wore to school and to Sunday school, and then back again to the more careful pressing of the hotel's laundry; and I remember that all his shirts worn to Sunday school at the Anglican church up the hill, upper-side from the Paynes Bay Beach, were made of silk. And that is why I am attracted now to the material of his tie and of the shirt he is wearing. They bring into greater focus, after forty-fifty years, those Saturday afternoons of borrowed books, and eating black pudding and souse, which his Old Lady made only on Saturdays, before she faced the mountain of hotel laundry. And of watching the sea, and hearing the waves and the sizzling of the hot clothes-iron travelling over the white shirts which the tourisses wore, and over the white shirts which the Vicar of the church upper-side of the beach wore to his secret-society meetings, the Masonics, as John's mother called them. "That is where he does-drink rum and eat corn-beef sangwiches with the Headmaster and the tourisses in the hotels, who happen to belongst to these same blasted secretive Masonics," John's Old Lady used to tell me. The stiffness in the neck of his collar and his cuffs, on this cold afternoon, is the same deal-board stiffness as I have seen him wear in his khaki shirts when he was in the Lower School, the same as I have seen in his white shirts when he was in the Upper School, the same as I have seen his Old Lady wash and iron. I cannot see his shoes. The room in which we are sitting, waiting for John to have me call the barman to come from behind the bar, is too dim for me to see under the table, which has a round, shiny, black top, and the dimness in this room,

the light from the bulbs, their glow and the red wall-
paper and the polished brass railings, is warm; and even
though the brass has been polished hours before, it
has a fragrance of affection and warmth and Brasso,
just like the feeling I have every Christmas Eve when
the tree is being trimmed with blue lights that wink,
and the presents are lying on the carpets, and incense
and candles are burning in soft anticipation; that smell
of love, of success, of life, that smell of warmth that
locks out all anxiety. Even the anxiety of hours spent in
cooking the turkey, and the short space it takes to
devour it, and strip it down to its bare bones. After it is
devoured, the more natural smell of love is then mixed
with a different kind of anxiety. In this room there are
paintings of the landscape of this country and this city
of Toronto, in the various whiteness of winter, with
thick unsullied snow in banks and on the branches of
trees which are white-limbed even without the colour
of winter. And in a strange way, now that my eyes are
accustomed to looking at them, these paintings make
the room even warmer, and I feel at home. But it could
be the light bulbs, small red balls under the bell-
shaped shades, or small white balls under the shades
of the fake Tiffany lamps. I cannot see his shoes, but I
imagine that they are black leather, since John always
wore black leather shoes. He was always fastidious in
dress. I sit facing him, and his face and his body become
the face and the body of the small boy years ago. I re-
member sitting beside him on the hard wooden bench

that had no back, in the elementary school, and stand-
ing beside him at the bus stop, five mornings in the
week, stiff in his khaki uniform pants, and his khaki
stockings pulled up to his large knees. His stockings,
like mine, had the school colours of blue and gold, in
the flashes, two pieces of ribbon attached to an elastic
band. They were worn on both legs, up to the knees.
On John's thin legs, his flashes attached to his garter
belts, when blowing in the wind, looked like two small
wings. But on Saturday afternoons, after the Library,
when I would sit in the verandah of his mother's house
when no breeze coming from the hills or off the sea
could cool the hotness of the day and the only wind was
in the smell of her cooking . . .

All of a sudden, cutting into my dreams of the past,
John begins to speak. "Time!" he says.

"Eleven? Twelve?" I tell him.

"Time for a drink, man!" he says.

"Twelve," I say. And we order our first drinks.

"No later?" he says, sipping.

"Looks like night, eh?"

"Midnight."

I drift off through the strength of my Scotch,
thinking of John's mother. She would be singing as
she moved the iron over the sea-island cotton shirt,
smoothened like a thin sheet of ice. She had a voice. It
was good enough for her to be the soloist in the District
of Paynes Bay Women's Choir of Voices. "To Be a
Pilgrim" was her favourite hymn. John's father did not

live with them. But he visited every other Saturday, when he brought pieces of pork and beef. Once, he brought a sheep's head, and water coconuts and, as usual, money for John's support, and money for John's mother's support, and money for John's school fees. That time of the sheep's head, with mutton attached to the head, and the eyes like pools of glass, the mutton soup that John's mother made, with dumplings of Robin Hood all-purpose flour mixed with cassava flour, was the Saturday John scored fifty runs for the school's cricket team, and clinched the Second Eleven Cricket Championship. We had the soup before and after his triumph.

John's father was a policeman, a constable. He was a constable for fifteen years. Nobody asked him why, but he gave everyone the reason. "You expect that it easy for a man like me to get three stripes on his blasted arm? With things the way they is, in this blasted country, and in this blasted constabulary? Answer me!" But no one dared.

So, he would come on his green Raleigh bicycle, and ring the bell making the first few notes of the current popular song which John and I would have listened to on the nightly Hit Parade, on Rediffusion Radio. All the songs were American songs. Billy Eckstine, Sarah Vaughan, Ella Fitzgerald, Nat-the-king-of-them-all Cole, Cab Calloway, and Louis Jordan were our stars. We listened to Bing Crosby and Frank Sinatra only at Christmas time to hear about white Christmases and "set-um-up-Joe," and compared *that* American sadness about drinking with the revelry of rum poured in larger quantities, without sorrow and loss of love, in all the rum-shops in our neighbourhood.

On his arrival, smiles would break our faces tightened against the closeness of the humidity on our bodies. And in our growing up, I always wondered why Saturday afternoons, when he visited, were always the hottest days of the week. The *ting-a-ling-ling* of the Raleigh's bell would announce him, and he would skip off the bicycle, and in the same motion bring it to its ticking halt, prop it against the side of the front-house, the front room of the house, and knock on the gate of the paling where John's mother had installed a bell against thieves and unannounced visitors and intruders. He would stand on the single coral-stone step leading into the kitchen and smile, waiting for her to say, "Come in, man! Why you ringing a bell?" He paid the rent for the house.

John would put the newly borrowed library book, *Treasures of the Oriental Caves*, face downwards, breaking its spine, and his mother would shout at him, and tell him to have "more respect for books and the knowledge inside the damn book"; and he would leave his index finger between the pages, and continue smiling. And John's mother would smile.

"But look at you!" she would say to John's father. She greeted him this way every other Saturday afternoon. Her greeting showed her love, faithful and constant during his long absences from her bed.

"How I look?"

"You look like you want feeding. You had anything to eat?"

"Look at my boy!" he would say to John.

And the shillings, with the Queen's smiling portrait scratched into their silver alloy, would come falling, one for me, four for John, and many more for John's mother.

Even when John's father was visiting, his mother would sing her favourite hymn, "To Be a Pilgrim."

"I'll fear not what men say . . ."

In my small mind, I would think she was trying to tell John and me something about the ways of mankind. Perhaps something said by the neighbours, her friends, in the shop where she bought groceries, standing in patient suffering for hours on Friday nights, talking out the business and secrets of the other women in the neighbourhood, their histories that went back for three generations sometimes. And behind her back, talking about her business. "Did you not know that that man don't sleep with her in the same bed every night? Yesss! He does-only-come-home once in a blue-moon." *"Prompt,* though!" "Yess. Every-other Saturday night he there, and by three o'clock Sunday morning, he gone!", while she watched the tricky iron-and-copper scales manoeuvre profits and losses, in the cunning hands of Mistress Edwards, the shopkeeper. All that time, all that talk, all that waiting while the talk walked through the crowded small shop. There, on

Friday nights, her waiting was appeased by the sweet voice of Ella Fitzgerald. *She* liked her, too . . . *Evening shadows make me blue* . . . "That man she have for a husband . . ."

"*I'll fear not what men say* . . ."

Sometimes, too, I would think she was emphasizing the words to include her resentment of the manager of the hotel, whom she swore did not pay her the full amount he collected from the tourisses to pay for getting their laundry done.

"*I'll fear not what men say* . . ."

"Those ten needles from the cobbler! What a thing, eh?" John says.

"And the tube," I say.

"Floating out, like a big, black Lifesaver, like the ones my uncle used to send in the parcels from Brooklyn-U.S.A., in the barrel of clothes and shoes, with the five-dollar money order. Always with the five Amurcan dollars in the money order, every-every month . . ."

"I had thirteen patches on the tire when she went out. Black and red pieces of rubber that I got from the man who repaired bicycles. We patched-them-on with Dunlop glue."

"And pump-up with a bicycle pump!"

He closes his eyes. To bring back more memories? To restrain the intervention of the strange atmosphere in the bar in which we are sitting now? And he gives a sigh. Not a heavy sigh, as people make when they are remembering sorrow in their past, or in the dark clouds. But a sigh, a soft exhalation of air to underline the happiness of that past.

"Let's have one more," he says. He raises his hand and Buddy comes towards us. "One for the road!"

"Can't walk on *one* leg!" I say.

"The time?" he asks again. "I have to go somewhere, but not now. Sometime . . ."

"You want to know?"

"The time?"

Men have come unnoticed into the bar. In our conversation that takes me across so many miles of sea, I do not notice the change in temperature in the room when they entered. Most of them are sitting on high stools, leaning on the bar. Buddy is busy. The room is warm. And friendly. And their talk is like a glow from a fireplace, like a low-hanging cloud. John looks around with some wonder at the peace in this bar. And then he rubs his hands together. I can feel the warmth in the room, just as I can feel it after I return to my house from my walks on Yonge Street to the Lake. Just as I feel after a long hot bath in December and January, with bubbles thick as clouds that hang in the sky when the rain is coming and make the water and the sea black and blue. We have been sitting for one hour now, and we are on our second Scotch. He has ordered Cutty Sark because, "Shit, the amount o' Cutty Sark, CS, that black people in the States, in Amurca drinks, shit, we could own the goddamn distillery!" He holds his glass with the thumb and index finger, the other three fingers of that hand, his right, cocked at an angle horizontal to the mouth of the short, stubby, cheap glass. "One thing about living in the States, we drinks the best and we eats the goddamn best, if you see what I'm saying!"

"Overrated," I say.

"Cutty? Or the States?"

"Overrated. Lemme show you the thing I was telling you about that I wrote, that I keep in my wallet, about never working again . . ." And I take from my wallet a piece of paper and hand it to him. It is a card two inches square, and laminated. It was dog-eared before I got it laminated at Grand & Toy. He takes it from me, holds it with the thumb and index finger of his left hand, and puts it close to his eyes and reads it. "'*December the twenty-sixth, nineteen hundred and eighty-six anno domini. I have decided not to work for anyone after this date.*' Is this *it*? Is this some kind o' poem?"

"It's a tract."

"Like in religious tract?"

"It is a political tract."

"What drove you to stop working? An accident? Sickness?"

"Nothing," I tell him.

"Come clean with me, goddammit!"

"A woman."

"Sexual harassment, then. You got that shit, too?"

"No. She died."

"Goddamn! I'm sorry, man. Let's have another drink. A double. Goddamn!"

He places the piece of cardboard face down on the round, shiny table on which our glasses have made interlocking rings of water. He traces a finger on one wet circle nearest to him, and ignores the message in my tract.

"Is *this* it?" he finally says, after he traces a few more figures in the wet rings. He makes one long line with the water.

"What do you mean, is this it?"

"Is that goddamn *all*?"

"This," I say, taking a photograph from my wallet, and placing it into his right hand, "this." He holds it again with his thumb and index finger, as if he is holding something precious, brittle, and old. The photograph is of a woman. I do not tell him who she is. It is a black-and-white. Aged now. To look like sepia. A crease on the glossy surface looks like a wound along the woman's face, a wound that will not heal. And the wound runs at an angle over her face, touching her breasts.

"Indian?" he asks.

"No."

"Looks Indian. Your daughter?"

"Not Indian."

"Your daughter," he says, not asking.

"A woman," I say.

"*Whose* goddamn woman?"

"My woman," I say. And he roars with laughter.

"You're robbing the goddamn cradle, man!" The other men and women in the bar raise their eyes in our direction and then lower them to their glasses and cigarettes.

"Goddamn!" he says.

"Chinese," I say.

"I'll tell you one thing! About the Chinese and Chinese food! God's gift to man. And something else! But what about the Chinese? Their food? Or something else you have in mind? A Chinese restaurant near here?"

"We're close to Chinatown."

"Goddamn! I hear they really know how to *take care* of a man! I love Chinese food! This your woman? Goddamn!"

"A friend."

"Friend, my arse! You're screwing her. *Fooping*. And at your age? Goddamn!" The men and women in the bar look up again. And then, when his voice fades, as the match to a lighted cigarette dies, they lower their heads and their eyes, and light fresh cigarettes and go back to their drinks, pretending they are not listening. "Tell me something. How old is this chick?"

"Her name is Lang."

"Ling?"

"Lang."

"Ling or Lang? Make up your goddamn mind! Like in Ming Dynasty? Ling or Lang?

"Forget it."

The barman brings us double Scotches this time, with no chaser. John has ordered them so. We sip in silence. Voices around us speak softly. A woman laughs, and her voice carries like a bell.

"I like this place," John says.

"She is why I stopped working," I say. He just stares at me. The woman laughs again.

"Lemme show *you* something," he says. "Lemme lay *something* on you." And he feels in his right trousers pocket, bulged big, taking the shape out of its custom-made fit, and extracts a billfold, about two inches thick. He takes out a plastic card holder, and, like a magician flicks his wrist and makes a flower grow, he makes the billfold become long, and longer, and it unfolds like a snake above the shiny, round table-top. Facing me through the plastic are credit cards. I have never seen so many different gold credit cards before: American Express, Visa, and MasterCard are visible, but there are many others. "Lemme show you something," he is saying, as he tries to turn the plastic snake over on its back. Backing and coinciding with each credit card is a Technicolor snapshot of a smiling face. "I call these my family." I count thirteen sections in the body of the wriggling plastic snake. Thirteen faces that do not all look white, but are all smiling, all healthy, most dressed in sweaters and brightly coloured blouses, and three in white shirts. "This is what I call the family." He holds his thumb on one framed photo in plastic at a time, and as he does this, he gives me the name. Those touched by his thumb are all girls, these children-members of his family. "From the same woman," he says. "From

Hyacinthe," he says, still holding his thumb on the plastic frame. "Faye." And he moves his thumb over the sectioned plastic snake, and says, "Roberto. Ricardo. And Umberto." The plastic becomes shorter, its body disappearing under his thumb. "Hanz. Gerhart. Franz. And Frederich." There are only three ribs left in the diminishing, fluttering plastic spine of the snake. Three faces. And then a fourth. "And Omawale Rashid." He says this with his eyes expressing great pride and love, holding the shortened snake now, with thumb and index finger, as he was holding his glass of Cutty Sark on ice. "The last o' my thrildren, a boy! From the woman I living with now." He places the two-sectioned snake flat on the shiny, round black table-top, with new water rings accumulated, and he says, "The three women I married-to. Best three women in the whirl! Hyacinthe, the *parlez-vous* woman. Isabella Maria Groppi, the Eye-talian. And Maude, the German *frauleene*!" Like a man who has accomplished a brilliant trick of magic, hypnotizing his audience into profound silence of disbelief, like a man who has triumphed over an opponent at a poker game of five-card stud, he fixes the plastic frames back into the palm of his hand, snaps the billfold shut, and pushes it back into his right trousers pocket. The magic is over. "Tell me about *your* family," he says, sipping his Scotch, pleased with his performance.

"I don't have one."

"Don't have a family? Every man have a family! Even if it's a rotten family. What you been doing? All this time, in this place, what you been doing? Wasting time with all these beautiful broads I see walking-'bout Toronto? I see them even in the hospital. No family? A man have to have a family, some kind o' family. I show you mine. Where yours is?"

"I don't have a family."

"Goddamn! I kinda figured as much from the way you talk, as if you're talking to somebody who isn't there. And the way you answer questions. You answer all my questions with another question. I happen to know from my work as a therapist that a man who does-live by himself which you say you does-do, which is not the same thing as living alone, mind you! But a man who lives by himself is a man who don't find it necessary to talk or answer questions. Or feel he should. Now, take a man like me. Accustom to so many pickneys round the goddamn house, a man like me is a man that can't stop talking. But I was talking, talking, talking from since I was small. You know that. So, no wonder I like studying people and psychology. You *don't* have a family? Never wanted one? So, who is this Chinese broad in the photograph that is cracked along the face? Who is she?"

"She not a broad!"

"Hey, hey, hey! Lady, then."

"*Was.*"

"What the fuck . . . ?"

"A woman," I say.

"In all the years you spend in this place, and no family? And only one picture of a Chinese woman in

63

your wallet that's faded and cracked? This is *all* you have to show for all that time, that you been walking-'bout the streets of Toronto? This Chinese woman would gotta be something more than just a woman!"

"A woman."

"I *know* she is a woman. But it got to be more!"

"What is the time?" I say.

"Time?"

"The hour?"

"You live here. Not me!"

"You remember *Galilee?*"

"And skinning scuffings?"

"Diving-off . . ."

"And the scuffings we used to skin, diving-off the side of *Galilee?* And diving into the sea? And in all that time, you couldn't swim!" He laughs again. And the men and women in the bar, now beginning to get full, look at us, smile at our words they cannot understand, and go back to their own joviality, the clinking of glasses and the flicking of cigarette lighters. "*Galilee*, your uncle's boat, was as big as a schooner."

"My aunt sold the boat to another fisherman when my uncle drowned. And that evening when they brought him in, swelled-up with the water in his body, he looked so big and so much younger, like a wrestler. And when they lay him down on the sand, I was sure that one of his fishermen-friends was going to stand on his stomach and force-out the water through his mouth. But I think they only took him in a hired car

64

straight to the undertakers, and left him there for two or three days, before they brought him back home. When they brought the body back home, they laid-him-out in the front-house on a thing that looked like two folding chairs, and he was in the coffin, a mahogany coffin that the joiner had-made, with silver things, ornaments all round the box. He didn't look like the same man they dragged-out the sea that evening. I always wondered why he looked so young, younger when he was dead, than when he was living and fishing and running up and down the beach in the early mornings, exercising. And then at the funeral . . ."

The laughter of the two women rises, and I stop talking. I can hear cars splashing along the street outside. In here it is warm and rich with a lighting like in a church just before evensong.

"Yes, but before the funeral, you remember how they laid-him-out in his black serge suit that he used to wear to funerals and weddings and lodge meetings, and while he was the deacon in the Nazarene Church? I can see him laid-out in that black suit, in that coffin, with his face looking more blue than black, as if they had bathed the body in water with ashes in it, or had-rubbed blue powder in his pores in his face. He looked more bluer than black, to me, than the black of his natural skin when he was running up and down the beach exercising in the mornings at dawn, doing his morning exercises and calisthenics. Wonder why black men of his complexion always look so blue when they are dead?"

"The blues, must be . . . The dirty blues!"

"Funerals back-then was such a lovely occasion, with the thrildren coming in the front-house of the house, and standing-up round the coffin, looking down into the coffin, through the oval hole that was always in a coffin at the top part, to see the dead. He had-on his favourite tie-pin pinned to his black tie, the tie-pin made out of tortoise shell. He had one black tie in all his life, for funerals and christenings. And one black suit, for funerals, weddings, Services-of-Songs and lodge meetings. But it was the smell of the water the undertakers had-bathe him in, after he was dead, the water that has the smell of lavender, that I remember. I remember the lavender water. And the smell he had when he was dead. A smell like camphor balls he used to put in the inside of the pockets of his serge suit to keep-away the moths. What is the name of the sprig of flowers they had in his lapel? Something old-something lace? Old woman's lace? Married-women's lace? Whatever the name is, it was, it looked like a sprig that was still growing on a branch. Everything else was dead except that piece of lace, that flower that my aunt had-picked and had-put in his lapel. But it wasn't like a funeral, a real funeral like the ones we sang at in the choir of the Cathedral on Friday afternoons before school was lay-by, and on Saturday afternoons. This funeral of my uncle was more like a Service-of-Song. And the moment his fishermen-friends enter the house, and look at him, peaceful, and stretch-out on his back, and quiet in his coffin, and *dead*, they start-up singing 'Those in Peril on the Sea.' It was suitable for a man dead or drowned at sea, like during the War. And they followed this with 'The Day Thou Gavest, Lord, Is Ending . . .'"

"Is *ended*! *Not* ending."

"*The day thou gavest, Lord, is ended . . .*"

"*The darkness falls at Thy behest*," John says in a voice as if he is singing.

And I take up the next line: "*To Thee our morning hymns ascended . . .*"

"*Thy praise shall sanctify our rest.* Hymn four-seven-seven. In *Hymns Ancient & Modern*," John says, imitating the sonorous voice of the Vicar whose words came through his nostrils, and then John, as if he is still the Vicar, conducting the ceremony for the Burial of the Dead, at the side of the grave, intones, "*Man that is born of a woman hath but a short time to live, and is full of misery. He cometh up and is cut down, like a flower . . .*"

"*Like a flower.* I wish I knew the name of that white flower."

"*And is cut down like a flower . . .* ," John continues, and he catches the spirit of a funeral and the ceremony for the Burial of the Dead in the small graveyard, amongst stones, falling headstones, and rich, tall growth of grass and no growing flowers except those in bottles and vases, beside the small Anglican church on the hill near Paynes Bay beach. And he is the small boy in the choir, dressed in the black cassock with the white ruff round his neck on which hangs the large silver cross; and we are singing. "*We thank Thee that Thy Church unsleeping . . .*"

"He was laid-out all that morning, Thursday morning, until the evening, when the men and his fishermen-friends full-up the house, and start the Service-of-Song for the dead, and the oldest fisherman was the chairman of the Service. The drinking and singing, singing as they went-through three jimmy-johns, a gallon each, of dark rum, as they went-through almost all the appropriate hymns in the book of *Hymns Ancient & Modern*, and my aunt lowered the wicks in the kerosene-oil lamps and the house was *plunge* in darkness, and the singing rose and got sweeter and mournful, and my God, the next evening, the Friday, at the funeral in the church at the service, all that black; black dress and black suit and black hats, and mauve; and the choir in black and the Vicar in black, and the skies I remember them was black too, just like the water at the shore where *Galilee* was resting on its side, up the beach, as if it *knew* where its captain was; and when those fishermen and his friends and cousins lowered him in the grave, the last thing was his wife, my aunt, who threw the flower, the same kind like the one that was in his lapel, on the coffin just before the last shovelful of dirt hit the top o' the coffin in such a loud sound, my God . . . that was the end. Then, the weeping."

"Jesus Christ!" John says. And, still standing in his black cassock, with the choir, in his mind, bringing this back, makes the sign of the Cross on his chest. His index finger of his right hand touches his expensive custom-made suit, at four dotted points.

The bar is quiet. Dead. Our voices have killed the chatter. Some eyes are turned in our direction. The barman is looking at us, wondering. And without request, he comes with two double Scotches on his brown, round plastic tray. The woman who had laughed now starts to cough. The bar returns to its silence.

"Where you was going when I bounced-into you?" John says.

"Nowhere."

"A man have to go *somewhere*. You can't just be walking and not going nowhere! You can't be just going from one place to the next, and not going *anywhere*! You must have some direction, even if only in your mind. A man just don't walk that way. You just can't walk from one spot to another spot, and still not be going anywhere! Goddamn!"

"Every day, at the same time, in any kind of weather, I leave my house and walk down Yonge Street heading straight for the Lake, and back from the Lake up again on Yonge Street and back to my house, walking the streets, seeing people passing, and sometimes, I try to smile with them . . ."

"I heard these words before!"

"I can't remember where they come from."

"From a song."

"They come to me when I walk."

"Goddamn!"

"I walk this street outside there, day in and day out, and I still can't rightly say I am going anywhere. I pass stores. I know that. I pass the same stores in winter as I pass in the summer, the spring, the fall. All the time. I see people . . ."

"Smiling and saying hello," John says, trying to remember. "Watching people passing by? Why won't it come back, this goddamn song? I know a song with words like these."

"Not always the same people. But people just the same. I see faces that I do not know, and I see people who are not related to me, except that, like me, they are people too, and nobody that I pass as I walk day in and day out knows me or recognizes me and I don't recognize anybody or know anybody . . ."

"Goddamn!"

". . . there is nothing, nothing that I see that has any bearing, any relation, any connection to me. Did you know that not *one* street in this city has a similar name to *any* street back home? So, I don't even see *that* connection."

"You're nothing but a walking ghost."

"I look in store windows and in stores, and I see my reflection in the glass, and a funny thing, just a few minutes before I bounced-into you, it crossed my mind to consider going back home."

"Back home? Man, there ain't no goddamn home back home!"

70

"Perhaps. But just to sit on the beach and spend my time looking out into the sea, at the tourist ships and the cruise-liners and the inter-island schooners, if they still have schooners, and the fishing boats. Perhaps buy-back and recondition *Galilee* and do a little fishing myself."

"But you can't even goddamn swim, fella! What kind o' fisherman you would make?"

"Most fishermen can't swim. That's why so many drown."

"That's for goddamn sure! Like your uncle!"

"True. There's nowhere to go for me. In this city, or back home."

"Take me, for an instance. Now, I am a man who live in the goddamn States, after knocking-'bout for years in Europe, France, Croatia, Belgium, Italy, *Deutschland-uber-alles*, Wess Germany and East Germany, now just-plain-Germany. But after a while, I got goddamn fed-up with European cultures and civilization, 'specially their goddamn *hot-cuisine*, where you hardly have enough food on your goddamn plate to fill a' ant! But the Germans? Gimme the goddamn Germans, the Nazzis, anytime! They like a lotta food and bittle that's heavy. Not this *hot-cuisine* like the French and the *parlez-vous* woman. So, I leave Brooklyn in New York where all of us settle at first, and I head straight for the goddamn South, in the heart of Dixie, y'all! Got my ass outta Brooklyn quick! Too many Barbadians and Jamakians living there now. I can't stomach any more reggae and

Barbadians with their spooge-songs and all that goddamn noise! All that noise. So, I high-tail my ass down South, y'all, to face the *real* thing! The real McCoy. And that's where I learn to make a man of myself. In the goddamn South. As a goddamn black Dixiecrack! I am a black Dixiecrack. If you see what I mean. In the South, they say a man is not a man if he be black, but I found myself as a man in the goddamn South, and made something of myself as a *black* man. I make sure I behave *and* talk as a Wessindian-black and *not* as an Amurcan-black. If you see what I am saying. Right there in the heart o' Dixie, I live a more better life than any black man or Wessindian in Brooklyn, than I did when I was hustling in Brooklyn-New York. I'll tell you something. I'll tell you what I mean. After I leff Europe, divorce three times, from three different wives, and with them behind me, I tried to practise the profession of a psychiatrist in the States. The States is a big place that likes big people, big ideas, and that take big risks. I am a big man. I live big. A man could hide in the South. And that is exactly what I did. I couldn't as a black man, playing around with therapy and psychiatry, hide in Brooklyn-New York. Tummuch goddamn Barbadians and Jamakians willing to report my arse to the Man! And since I did not have my three wives with me, 'cause they was back in Europe, I tried to piece-together my fucked-up life, what was leff of it. So, I opened a little clinic, just an office, a hole in the wall, and I took a big risk, practising as a therapist. You can take big risks in the States. My therapist business took off. And then, I had the nerve to set myself up as a psychiatriss. You're goddamn right! A psychiatriss. Well, really, as a therapist. Shit, what do I really know about being a therapist? But you gotta take risks. Big risks, big success. And bigger bucks. Or land in jail. But me? You'd be goddamn surprised what a little jazz-up furniture, in a' office, fancy telephones, those old-fashioned ones from England in the nineteenth century, like the ones you see in books, or in murder movies with Sherlock Holmes and Dickens, things you come across in library books. You would burst your ass laughing. But this ain't no goddamn laughing matter, this is taking risks. Big risks in a country with a big vision. My ass could be in jail, in a federal penitentiary any morning, even tomorrow, if I slip-up, if they catch me practising without a licence. But Amurca is Amurca; and only in Amurca, they say, anything can happen. After that, I had my hand in a little real estate, a venture or two, and after a few years, with one thing and the other, and not having a real-estate licence, I made a little money, a few Amurcan *smackeroons*, and today I can't complain. Meanwhile, I take care of all my thrildren, every last one o' those bastards, *lovely* thrildren really. And the wives, too. Not that they make me pay alimony, 'cause I am here, and they are there. But I send the three o' them a little something, regular. By U.S. Postal Money Order. Have the bread to do it. Not that I goddamn like the idea of all this bread leaving the States for Europe. Goddamn!

I am an Amurcan. A Yankee. You seen my gold credit cards, when I showed you my family, didn't you? A man can live there. Amurca is Amurca. And the South is the best goddamn place for a man from the Wessindies, for a man like me to live. Not that my life was always like that, a bed o' roses. No sirree! Shit, I remember bathing with only cold water in the house, in the goddamn tap! For four goddamn months. And that wasn't in the summer neither! Motherfuckers disconneck the fucking heat. Motherfuckers disconneck the hot water. Every goddamn convenience a man needs to live conveniently by, the motherfuckers *offed.* Heat and hotness, and lights. Don't talk about the telephone! But I grit my goddamn teeth, swallowed my pride, and I stood underneat' that goddamn cold shower every morning at six, during the week. I stood like Hercules under that goddamn cold shower every morning at six as I say, "Fuck it!" and *dared* the motherfuckers to beat me, or have me buckle-under to them. Beat *me?* A man that grow up in Barbados, in the Wessindies, near Paynes Bay, by the beach where we had as role-models all those fishermen and men so strong and brave and goddamn poor that they would look a goddamn shark in the eye and say, 'Motherfucker, I am *the* man! You is mine!' Never. Never-once in my whole lifetime near the beach with that rubber tube we used to lay on in the sea, *never once* did I see any of those men, my father, your uncle, your father, my uncle, and a million cousins, second-cousins, third-cousins, cousins ten-times remove, *never*-goddamn-once did I hear that any o' those men beg for mercy! Did you? *Beg for mercy?* I stood under that goddamn frozen shower, grit my teeth, and call the motherfuckers 'motherfuckers'! But I did not beg for mercy."

"Strong men."

"Goddamn! What the Southerners like to call cowboys tough-as-hide, or role-models. They was goddamn role-models!"

"Strong men. Like my uncle."

"Like your uncle. God rest his soul."

"Poor men, too."

"That, too. But strong men. Like my father."

"And strong women to back-them-up!"

"Strong goddamn women! And this may surprise you now. But when I think of my three ex-wives that it was my goddamn privilege to be married-to, I take my hat off to each and every one of them, as role-models, 'cause those three broads was three goddamn strong women! Had to be!"

"Like your Old Lady."

"Like my goddamn Old Lady. God . . ."

". . . rest her soul."

"I showed you the snapshots, didn't I? This one of my Old Lady, I carry next to my Green Card, in a plastic thing . . . laminated? *Laminated.* Side-by-side."

"Like my note to myself. Did you get sick with pneumonia?"

"From what?"

"When the hot water was cut off in the winter?"

"I was embarrass. That was the only illness I suffer. Because of the way they stripped me of my basics and my conveniences. I almost sued their ass for the inconvenience. But I change my mind. I was glad, though, that I wasn't living with anybody, like a woman, 'cause to come home and have *that* thrown in my face by a woman, even if she was my wife, that would make me kick her ass! But I am not a violent man, normally. But it was *cold*! It was *co-o-o-ld,* Jack! I endured it. For four months, during one o' the coldest winters Brooklyn ever faced. And with the 'lectricity cut-off, you shoulda seen my goddamn freezer! We Amurcans like bulk, and buying in bulk. And we eat that way, too. So in my freezer I had me four turkeys for Thanksgiving and Christmas and the reunion of my ex-wives and family, the biggest goddamn turkeys you ever rested your two eyes on, and I had me some pork chops, and some steaks, salt fish, cow-foot and ox-tails; and a friend who me and him go hunting together sometimes, and once we catch a deer, so I had me some game in the freezer, from that deer after we skinned the son of a bitch. Got him with two shots. *Blam! Blam!* The goddamn blood! All that blood. But the meat was tender. Well, I couldn't cook it, and I couldn't bake it, and I couldn't goddamn boil it, neither. I had to throw it in the garbage, after I give-way the rest. To my landlady, and some Jamaikan neighbours. Goddamn!"

"I think you were embarrassed like I was . . . not being able to swim."

"So, what you think o' me, after all these goddamn years? You think I change? You haven't change much to me. Not really. A little grey, that's all. From that day on the beach. The same cool motherfucker! Eh, Timmy? But in a way you *have* change. A little. But I can't figure it out. And you walk that same street, what's its name, at the same time every day, and you telling me you're not going anywhere, or looking for chicks? Do you visit the girlie-shops, then? They have striptease joints here? Men our age, when we reach a certain age, and can't get it up no more, all we do, all we can do, is *look*. Looking don't cost nothing, man. And it don't kill. Or a little watching to remind you to remember when you was a strong man and *could* do it. It happens to the best of us. I think this is what you do, on your walks. You can confide in me, your oldest friend, and a man on the brink of sexual disaster of being able-only to look. Looking don't cost a penny. So, who is the Chinese chick? In your mind, or a real chick? So, where the hell you go, when you're walking that street outside there, is your business. Just be honest, brother!"

"You used to like to talk with an English accent at Combermere School. It got worse at Harrison College. I remember your English accent. You still have a little of it."

"You remember some real strange things!"

"I remember every thing. The day you had the cobbler in your foot, the day you lost your voice singing

77

"We Three Kings of Orient Are," the first time you came first, the day you made sergeant in the Cadet Corps, the day your uncle left on the ship for the States . . ."

"I remember your uncle's funeral, too. I remember the inner tube floating out. I remember trying to talk like an Englishman. Chermadene. And how you got a kiss before me. I remember dropping my accent when I got to university in England. Remember the boat I leff on. You remember the boat I leff on? And the well-wishes on the Pier Head that night? The *S.S. Antilles*? But I dropped the accent. Now, the only accent I use and like to hear, apart from Bajan, is the way Southerners talk. I would do anything to talk like a real Southerner."

"You sound like a black American."

"Like an African Amurcan, that's the new word for it. We dropped the goddamn hyphen in AfroAmurcan."

"Why didn't you learn French? Or German? Or even Eye-talian?"

"Was all that goddamn *parlez-vous* food. German? I didn't like *that* language. And with the Eye-talian, I didn't have to learn that, knowing already Latin and a little Spanish. Besides, you don't really have to know the language, if you know the woman . . . if you see what I'm saying! Remember? So, where did you go to university?"

"Trinity."

"You were *so* close to me, and didn't try to track-me-down? Trinity, Dublin? What a lovely place! Chermadene went to Trinity, too. I bumped into her in France."

"What is Chermadene doing?"

"It was a summer in France. She is who told me you were in Trinity. She went home and went into politics and law. I hear she is now the Governor General."

"Chermadene? The girl with the two braids?"

"Her Excellency!"

"Jesus Christ! We should have married Chermadene!"

"Both o' we? She never got married, though. But imagine, you were so close to me!"

"Trinity College, Toronto."

"*Not* Dublin? Well, you can't say you went to Trinity, if you don't mean Trinity, Dublin! I thought you were talking about the *real* Trinity."

"The real Trinity?"

"Father, Son, and Holy Ghost. The real Trinity," John says, and makes the sign of the Cross – this is the third time he has crossed himself – and he adds, anticipating that I am about to ask him why, "Something you pick up in Catholic countries, from Catholic women. I enjoyed London. How was *your* Trinity?"

"The only time in this country that I really enjoyed myself. Not every day. But three years outta forty-something. One-fifteenth of my life here. The only ones that I want to remember. I met the Chinese woman in those first three years, and ever since then . . ."

"Is she the same person in the snapshot? So, she's still alive then? How come she looks so young, like a child? She looks like twenty-two."

"She's sixteen. But she has no age . . ."

"She *can't* be! She's a *child*. You're into kiddy-porn, robbing the fucking cradle . . ."

"In the picture."

"You're still robbing the cradle."

"To me, she is the same person in the snapshot, and in my mind."

"Wait a cotton-picking minute! You confusing me. You are confusing someone who is dead with some-one who is still living? In my profession, this is a goddamn serious thing, man. Are you sure you talking about a living person? My question about where you go, and now this Chinese girl, is the same thing, in my profession."

"Let me tell you a story," I say. "It was at University. In Trinity. And the college was empty, emptying-out at this time, dead at this particular time, a Friday. On Fridays, *every* Friday, all of us students from the West Indies and who were not born here, and who didn't know anybody in the city, or in the University were like living deads. There was not even a person to sit down with and drink a rum. When we looked forward to the coming of Friday evenings and the stillness of Friday nights, meaning nothing more than just that, that dead peace and quiet, that deep, deep loneliness, some of us, big men, used to cry. It was another week-end filled only with studying and studies. There were no women. Women were out of the question. There were no West Indian women on the campus, and cer-tainly no black Canadian women, so at this time on a

Friday evening, panic came with dusk. There I was, far from home, when, if I was back home, at that time o' day, I would be sitting on the beach, or going to a picnic. And perhaps . . . *not* perhaps, *for-sure* I would be seeing some lovely girls walking up and down the beach. My room at the college was not the same as my home back home. I would be, at that time on a Friday evening, I would be lifting a crystal glass in the short arc and space from the table to my waist, then to my head, to my mouth and lips. The college was like a graveyard on Friday evenings. And then, all of a sudden, I was resurrected one Friday night. On that night in question . . . as I remember it . . . and remembering it now, years after, is like it was last night. I find that I live the past as if it is the present. They mean the same to me. At my age, I prefer the past. So, what I'm telling you . . . the story I am telling you about last night is really the same story as that Friday night, years and years ago. Understand? They're mixed into one." John has stopped drinking, to listen. "It was like a night of pure fantasy. But a night of poetry, and a landscape which, when my eyes touched it, buried me by its prospect in the dales and hills and undulations and certain cervices and secretions of its topography. All this was secret previously and hidden against any exploring I could have made, until last night. Fantasy and poetry. But I tell you that, when I surveyed the scene, I had to get down on my knees before God and ask Him for five minutes and mercy. I told Him, 'Lord, do not take this cup from me. Do not take it outta my hands until I have sipped the sweetness and the juices, down to the dregs . . .'"

"Dregs?" John says, his eyes riveted on the story. "God-*damn!*"

"It was like Sodom and Gomorrah. It was like Daniel in the lion's den, Ananias and Saphira, Adam and Eve. And the three red apples, Macintoshes they call them here. It was like Jonah in the belly of the whale. The seas parted, like the seas that rise-up and tumbled-over the bow of *Galilee* that tossed my uncle overboard. Those seas of that night's story were filled with sharks that kill, the seas that washed-him-in, big, bloated, and bulgeous . . ."

"Goddamn!"

". . . and as I tell you this story now, I was like a child that was starved of seeing food. I was seeing food for the first time. It was like seeing the great cricketer, Sir Frank "Tai" Worrell, a member of the three fierce W's. It was like seeing "Tai" late-cutting to backward-gulley so fine and so delicate that you almost missed the stroke and missed the ball if you had-looked too late. That, as you remember, is the definition and derivation of a *real* late-cut!"

"Goddamn!"

"Man, when I tell you that last night was like a song by Roberta Flack about the Reverend Doctor Lee, was . . ."

"Goddamn!"

"Reverend Doctor Lee was kneeling-down in front of the body of the sister in the church, facing that kind of temptation that only Satan could-have-*contrived* and created . . . Lang was that kind of sweet temptress!"

"Goddamn!" John says, cutting into my narrative with his exclamations of wonder, in a hissing-like sound, so that his voice would not travel to the other customers in the warm, dim, sweet-smelling bar. The bar is now filled with shopping bags and large parcels, gifts wrapped and bowed in the yuletide of the dying afternoon. All these women have those gifts lying at their feet.

"It was that kind o' temptation that only Lucifer could confer to ole Rev-and-Doc Lee. To Reverend Doctor Lee. Words I have do not contain fullness nor nuance of meaning to clothe that experience that I experienced last night with Lang. She was beautiful last night. Although she's dead, as I said. That land-scape that I was lying-down on. With her back flat to the mattress, her two legs like two pieces of sweet sugar cane. Her bubbies, those breasts, my God! Those luscious breasts, Lord have His mercy! And sudden-so, I started to think that children and infants and babies are the luckiest sons-o'-bitches in the world, *in the whole world*. They can feed and suck on the nipples of breasts and bubbies, at their beck and call. Lang was shy about that. But at the first sign of a scream, babies are afforded these nice, fat, juicy bubbies in their mouths, as a natural gift of birth."

"Goddamn!" John is twisting in his chair. I can see his sensual discomfiture in his wriggling.

"I really and truly asked God for five minutes. Out of my whole life. And then, I had to request of Him five more minutes. The cup of Lang is a gift that was placed at my lips containing too much responsibility. And a challenge. And when the second reprieve had run-out, I saw Lang strong and more beautiful. And I had to face my weakness, and my failing. I could not accommodate the burden it caused me. The burden of that fear of sterility. God, please lend me another five! It was an epic journey like in the poem *Paradise Regained* . . .

"Goddamn!" John says. "More like *Pardise Lost*!"

"I saw paradise last night. And I saw *Paradise Lost*. I had struggled to hold on to it, as it was moving away from me. Life and Lang. Moving out of reach, like a wave in the receding sea. My experience in this journey is limited. Fantasy and poetry. I had to use imagination. I bite it. I eat it. But I lost it. And then, I regained it. But Lang is stronger, so I lost it. And then, it was morning. Morning came as a relief. A night of pain from a toothache or a pain in the stomach, morning always saves you. Things look more real in daylight. And when morning broke, Jesus Christ, *Paradise* was *Regained* for the second time . . ."

"Goddamn!"

"I was fagged-out. The bed was soaking-wet. I had been suffering from a fever of impotent sexual journeying. An old man. The water poured off my body.

The parameters, the location, the environment, the circumstance, and the atmosphere itself, the meaning of the journey undertaken on that bed remained untouched, and it passed my understanding. Lang remained untouched and unconvinced. Goddamn! Man, it was still pretty. As beautiful and new an experience as a new shilling. Fantasy and poetry."

"Goddamn!" John says.

He says this as if he himself is going through the exertion of the narrative, as if he himself has endured the details of my journey over the landscape of the story.

"Are you dreaming this story for my benefit? Like, where are you coming from? She's dead, man! She's dead!"

"All during this time, I could not concentrate on anything else. It is only smells that I was smelling, scents that I was scenting, juices I was tasting, spasms I'm spasmadizing and feeling, vibrations I vibrating, vibrations, pillow, mattress and springs, the experience that I experienced last night. I remember antique furniture all of a sudden. For no reason. I remember old, expensive plate with flowers painted round the rim, in gold and blue. I remember crystal and silver and lace. I remember champagne. I remember white wine. I remember paisley. I remember silk from India or China or from worms and cotton in the island. I remember brassieres. I remember lace. I remember the leather in her boots. I remember a bath towel thick as a steak from Bigliardi's on Church

Street. I remember a white cotton dress that hangs from her body. I remember coffee from the hills of Kenya, and the Blue Mountains of Jamaica, perked and jerked. I remember the flash of a red pair of underwear that was transparent, that you could see through, delicate as the web a spider is spinning, lace that you could punch with your eyes and see through from here, all the length, all the time to the coming of an orgasm. I remember her eyes were as thin as a slit of glee pressed tight in anticipation, and full of tears. I remember the beauty of her skin. I remember a tattoo on her left bubbie, her left breast. And I remember the tattoo high on her thigh, near to her . . . her, and seeing that it would have to have been *shaved* for a tattoo to have been placed so delicately and precariously *there*, and I touched the tattoo and I touched *there*, like a man grasping the straw of his surviving rescuer. The first tattoo and the second tattoo were both of red roses with two leaves of green, each. I remember the dunlopillo, the foam-rubber mattress of her vibrating bed. I remember incense. *Tisiang Tsang incense from Beijing, China.* I remember hearing my name called-out in chilling, plaintive, forcing screams of someone drowning, like how my uncle was drowning, someone going-down, down, down, in a voice that hasn't much strength left in it from the struggle of surviving, a voice not too loud, because breath and life are at a premium. I remember the depths of desperation and desolation. And the heights of righteousness. I remember, I remember, I remember."

"Goddamn! *God*-damn! God-*damn!*"

"I remember yesterday, as clear as if it is happening now. Here. Last night is tonight. *Now.* But. There. Last night. It was like a trough of glory and damnation."

"Goddamn!"

"I tell you that it was a jewel. From now-on, I may not live, may not be alive for *one* more day, and don't want to be, to be able to tell my testimony of confession to anybody else but you . . ."

"Goddamn!"

"I was fagged-out."

"You was *fucked*, brother!"

"I can't remember when I started-out on this journey. And I can't remember when it came to its end. I can't remember anything more. Perhaps what I just described to you is a dream or a fantasy. Dreams and fantasy at my age are the same as fact. Something like being able to make an imagination come true, like wanting to be with the woman from China. Perhaps what I just narrated is nothing more than what my mother calls a "friction" of my imagination. I use it to light the loneliness I live with. The boredom. Nothing so good in real life has ever happened to me. Not even in a dream."

"Ain't no dream, brother. You was *fucked!*"

"It is a dream. Take it as a dream."

"Dream, my black ass! You was fucked, brother. Goddamn!"

"It could be a dream."

Outside, on the white street, the darkness of night is falling. The lights in the bar are now visible in the changing light. The sharp, bright, blinding reflection of the snow outside is now turned into the soft, short, glowing movement of flames from matches and cigarette lighters. Voices are soft. The sound of drinks, glass and ice and bottles placed on tables, is as decorous as white wine served in crystal and placed on a mat on a table-top, on the silent, almost noiseless linen tablecloth. A woman gives off a giggle, remembering perhaps a happy moment in the long day at the office, which has ended just a few moments ago. A man speaks in a voice as seductive as his hand which passes stealthily over the colours in her winter shawl. She removes the hand travelling like a spider. The blood-warming colours of her shawl and the comfort in the bar are disturbed, but only for a moment, when a man and a woman enter, and the door is left open. Outside is the evening. Time has changed through the passing of hours, how many hours I do not know, and John is not interested; but it is still sharp and bright and blinding on Yonge Street, the streetlamps hit against the undying whiteness.

"This Cutty Sark ain't doing nothing for me," John says. "What's the time? Why don't we try something else?"

"Gin," I say.

"Martinis?"

The lights make all the faces in the bar visible now. There are women who sit together in groups of three and four, taking drinks that are thick and white, and some that have slivers of fruits, cartwheels of orange and lemon and lime, and they remind me of the trials with drink at this time of year that are not resorted to when January comes, and of the avalanches of food, and the desperation of figure and form that must be squeezed into dresses of black and red and green, which had been gift-wrapped in the best intentions of gold and silver paper, now that the holidays are spent. Men, who do not have the same obsession, drink fast. They throw the other caution, *si vous buvez, ne prenez pas le volant*, to the cold winds. They ignore the Liquor Control Board of Ontario, and the police, disregarding in one gulp and puff the bold-typed mortal scare on two sides of their Player's and Dunhills – Cigarettes cause cancer. *La cigarette cause le cancer* – and they send out clouds of smoke from their lips, and these float in the reddish, warm light while they cough. All this is taking me back to the beach, when we two men, young boys then, sat un-smoking on the sand the colour of the conch-shell, ignorant that a cigarette in French is feminine, and the cancer it causes is masculine. We sat, then, looking into those clouds above the green sea, seeing forms and imagining shapes in them that quench our anxiety for departure. Our plans were as loosely shaped as those clouds, and these puffs of cigarette smoke floating above and around us. I think of years ago, but in this country, when I was in the same shape as John with no money, and the Gas and

Electricity people turned their services off; and of that one time, one week before Christmas when I had to dress in suit and long-sleeved sweater, winter coat, scarf, gloves, and Russian-bear winter hat, two pairs of ugly grey construction socks with red bands around their tops, stomping from one room to the next. I walked up and down like a soldier marching in shivering fear on a battlefield in a similar theatre of war to those that Napoleon fought in and lost. After this exhaustion, I remained colder than if I had been outside in the glistening street with vapours of clouds spewing from my mouth. In this room, in this bar, the softness of the lights and Christmas on our breaths warm me and join me again, after all these years, to that afternoon when the two of us sat on the sand and the warm sea water cleaned the grains of conch-shell sand from between our toes, and we looked at the whiter clouds playing over the green fortune-telling sea, up into the blue skies. I see things now as if for the first time. The lights come alive and I can see them now, although they have been burning the whole time.

"What do you do?" John asks. It takes me a while to realize that he is speaking. "What do you do?"

"Now?"

"These days."

"What do you mean?"

"These days, what do you do?"

"Killing ants," I tell him.

"Killing ants?"

"They're eating-down my house."

"So, you walk around in your house, killing ants with a spray-gun? What kind o' ants? Red ants? Brown ants? Ants that sting, stinging ants?"

"Wood-ants."

"Goddamn! Run that by me one more time. You. Walk around your house. Killing wood-ants. Goddamn! Is this what this country is doing to you, brother? At your age? After all these years? You don't know where you're going when you walk out on the street, you say. You walk around your house, benning-down, looking for goddamn ants to kill, you say. And you say they're eating-down the house? And you talk about this Chinese woman who I don't know if she is dead, or alive. Don't you have to find the direction the ants're going in *first*, before you can kill them?"

"Picture me, since you're so interested . . . There I am, sitting down in a chair, with a large can marked 'Black Flag,' and . . ."

"*Black Flag?* Goddamn!"

". . . and with a Scotch and soda in my other hand, and I find myself just watching and waiting. I find myself sitting in that chair, looking at the patterns in the carpet, at the patterns, like knots in the floorboards, waiting, and *sudden-so*! I see a son of a bitch! A' ant! And I uncover the top of my Black Flag easy, easy now, eeeasy . . . and I look again to see if the knot in the floorboard is an ant. Or if it is part of the pattern, or if the pattern in the carpet has changed from my eyes focusing on it. And I look hard . . . eeeassy, easssy, 'cause the son of a bitch has ears and eyes, and the son of a bitch plays tricks, plays dead, and tries to fool me. And when the son of a bitch moves, *squish!* Got it! The son-of-a-bitch starts wriggling and walking in circles!"

"God-*damn!*"

"And I have to hold my Scotch and soda far from the sprays, in case this damn Black Flag has-in something that is detrimental to my drink."

"*Black Flag!*"

"Black Flag, with a flag attached to a mast, like any flag you see flying on buildings. The Stars and Stripes for instance, or the Canadian flag, the red maple leaf. But Black Flag is a *black* flag, not of a country, but with 'black flag' written in big, white capital letters on the can."

"*Black Flag.* Goddamn!"

"*For ants. Ant, cockroach and earwig killer, with chlorpyrifos. Continuous killing action for sixty days.*"

"You memorized all that?"

"Yeah."

"Sixty days? Goddamn!"

"Continuously killing those sons-o'-bitches!"

"But what is a' earwig?"

"I never looked it up in the dictionary."

"I could tell you about cockroaches. In Brooklyn . . . well, no need to say more. But I have never come-across earwigs. Cockroaches I know. In Brooklyn, goddamn, they be the most multitudinous motherfuckers on earth! You kill one, and you see five more. You bring-in the exterminators with their fancy equipment for killing roaches, and they kill hundreds. And the min-ute they take your cheque and pack-up their high-tech gadgets and drive-off, Jesus Christ! Then, you *really* see cockroaches! In their millions! Goddamn! As if the roaches love the exterminator fluid! But you and your can o' Black Flag . . ."

"In the summer, I am sitting on the front steps, watching people pass. All kinds of people. Women pass. Men pass. I watch women pass, watching women walking and holding hands with women, men with men, and kissing . . . yes, kissing! Men making passes at women. Prostitutes at the corner . . ."

"I'll be goddamned! *Where* is your house situated? Such lovely broads as I see during my short stay in Toronto, and some even at the hospital, such pretty broads kissing one another? Goddamn waste o' flesh!"

". . . and men passing and holding hands, and kissing, and sometimes . . ."

"Getouttahere! Goddamn! And you holding-on to your can o' Black Flag!"

". . . and if I take my eyes off the sons-o'-bitches . . ."

"The women? Or the wood-ants?"

"And if I take my eyes off the sons-o'-bitches for one second! Those goddamn wood-ants, as you would say. The ants, I mean. And when I stop looking at the two women kissing in front of my railing, a *stream* of ants, marching in line. Big ones. With little bags attached, their guts full of the dust of wood from eating-down and eating-up my blasted house!"

"Wood-ants do not eat wood!" John says.

"To me, they do!"

"And out comes your can!"

"Goddamn right!"

"And *squirt-squirt*!"

"Kill the motherfuckers!"

"With your big Black Flag can in your hand!"

"*Continuous killing action for sixty days!*"

"What do you do with them, after you kill them?"

"Nothing."

"Leave them where you kill them? You don't bury them? With a killing action for sixty continuous days, you could have a mountain of the motherfuckers in the house, encouraging other motherfuckers. A real big ant-hill. Shit, brother, you gotta do *something*, some-goddamn-thing with those ants that you kill!"

"I am a man, sitting, looking at the pattern in the carpets and the knots in the hardwood floor, looking, waiting for ants. And when I see one, *squirt*! Out goes the son of a bitch!"

"Any cockroaches?"

"No cockroaches."

"What about rats? And mice?"

"Occasional. But I live in Rosedale."

"The Black Flag can out-out those, too?"

"Never tried. But I'll think about it, though. For I am a man who sits in a chair, with a Scotch and soda in one hand and my can in the other, waiting for those sons-o'-bitches to move. If they *just* move, I got them. Let a' ant *move*, and I gottem!"

"Goddamn!"

"And I have started to make a study of ants. After a while, you get to know them, and you find yourself studying them. Liking them, almost. How they move. When they come out. When they are fooping. When they are having little baby ants, their children. They sure have a sense of the multiplication tables! How they send their messages of danger to one another. And do you know something? I believe they have sense and intelligence and that they send out vibrations and S-O-S's. Because I can kill one, and quick-so, three or four would run-out from under a piece of wood, run to the ant that I squirted with Black Flag, and scamper, just like real people running from a fire. I have been studying ants."

"Goddamn, I say! All I can say is *goddamn!*"

"Ants."

"Reminds me. You still do a lot o' reading? Like we used to do back home, in the olden days, when me and you used to have reading-races? We went to the Public Library every Saturday morning, early-enough before I had to go and play cricket, and how we used to bring back four books each; and sometimes, if the librarian was in a good mood, she would let us take-out six? Adventure books, mysteries, Agatha Christie, murder stories, English novels – Jane Austen and so forth –

history books, all kinds o' books. You still read as much? Well, if you still do . . ."

"Five books a week. There's a library round the corner from my house. But not in the last five years."

"Well, if you still used to, you woulda come-across a book with a French name . . . lemme see if I can remember the name in French. I think it was . . . lemme see . . . something like . . . *autobus? Autobahn?* . . . *Auto-something! Auto-auto-auto* . . . *Auto da Fé?* Yes, *Auto da Fé!* Ever read *Auto da Fé?*"

"Never heard of it."

"You have to read it. Ever heard of Elias Canetti?"

"An Eye-talian?"

"Bulgarian. Born in Bulgaria with Spanish and Jewish parents. Lives in London. And I don't mean London-Ontario!"

"The Mother Country's London."

"Your obsession with killing ants remind me of Klein. Now the author, Elias Canetti, has this Klein fellow obsessed by books the same way you're obsessed by ants. I only read the first hundred and seventy-three pages, out of four hundred and twenty-eight. But I came-across this novel, *Auto da Fé*, in 1979, in Italy. No, in Germany. Klein is a strange man. You remind me of Klein, one crazy son of a bitch. Klein liked books like you like ants. Not that a' ant is similar to a book, but in my profession we call them the same thing, this obsession, a' obsession of fatalistic proportions. Talking plain, and not as a professional, I would say that an obsession is nothing more than love gone so far that it turn-into hate and hatred. You can't tell one from another. Not that you are crazy, or becoming crazy. But you should watch yourself. These blasted ants, and the amount o' time you spend looking at them, with that Black Flag in your hand. You may very well have an obsession with ants, like Klein had an obsession with books."

"I never thought ants were like books. To me, it is getting-rid of pests."

"Symbolically. Well, metaphorically speaking, also. Anyhow. Take Klein. I just happen to remember, word-for-word, a serious passage dealing with obsession. This is the passage whiching I am trying to remember . . ."

"You always had a good memory. I remember that you were best at remembering the translations from Virgil *Aeneid* and Livy XXI and Caesar *Gallic War*. You always could memorize anything."

"'*Quidquid id est, temeo Danaos donas ferentes.*' Remember that?"

"'I fear the Greeks when they bring gifts'!"

"You're not senile yet, neither! You remember Hannibal? And how Hannibal crossed the Alps with his columns of elephants? '*Hannibal, in occulo altero Alpam transgresserat cum impedimenta*'? And that is something that up to today the Eye-talians can't face, nor accept. Historically speaking, and psychologically too, that *Hannibal cross the fucking Alps!*"

"Pun intended?"

"Pun in-fucking-tended!"

"But you were talking about Klein."

"Oh, yes, Klein. No pun intended. I hope you don't mind the comparison. Here it is. I am trying to remember it from memory, but it won't come back. I'll just tell you the story of Klein. Klein was a man who would walk up and down in front of his books in his library, calm as a cucumber, and sudden-so, he would start making these strange noises like a man going mad, and all of a sudden would stop walking, and stand at attention. Just so. Come to a full stop. Just as strange, he would get up on a ladder, and climb to the blasted top o' the bookshelf o' books. And guess what next Klein would do? Klein takes out one book, leaf-through a few pages, and puts the book inside his briefcase. He gets back down, and starts walking up and down the library again. Klein stops. Thinks. Studies himself. And then, *blam!* Pulls out another book. One. Two. Three. Four. Five books. One of these books was giving him trouble, so he takes this book, and *blam!* shuts it hard. The five books was heavy-heavy in the briefcase, and guess what Klein did next. Up again on the fucking ladder, *with* the briefcase o' books. Back up to the top, to the last rung of the ladder. With the briefcase of five big books. Up at the top. He starts taking out the five books. One by one. One. Two. Three . . . and while taking out the fourth, to put it back into the shelf, his blasted foot got tangled-up in the ladder. The shift o' weight and books. And what you think happened next to Klein?"

"He put-back the other four books?"

"He fell-off the fucking ladder and broke his ass!"

"Klein did?"

"Klein did."

"Klein died?"

"Nearly."

"That's serious."

"That's what I been telling you about holding a can o' Black Flag and killing ants."

"Goddamn, as you would say!"

"But you may be all right. You ever fall-off the steps in your front yard? Or the stairs inside your house? By the way, was the ants black, or red?"

"Black, and fat, and lumbering. And when I squirt them, Jesus Christ, you should see the juice, the stuff coming-out of them! The ants are black."

"Just like the cobbler that was in my heel that afternoon, when we were sitting-down on the beach. Cobblers in Barbados're black. Ants are brown. You don't have to worry about falling off steps or stairs, then."

"I had a fall once, though."

"Going after a' ant? Off your front steps?"

"Off the bed."

"Goddamn! Did the Chinese chick throw you outta bed? Goddamn! This is getting to be more serious! A chick did that to you? At your age? I told you about trying to foop young women!"

"It was after I had-seen these ants crawling-over the pattern in the carpets, and stopping-dead and pretending to be knots in the hardwood floor; but I spotted the sons-o'-bitches as ants, anyhow! So, any-how. I had-gone to bed, and . . ."

"Alone? Or with the Chinese woman?"

"At my age? *Alone.* I had-gone into bed, and was dreaming, and it was a good dream I . . ."

"A wet-dream?"

"A dream. You dream a dream in the night, and then in the morning you can't remember what you dreamed? One o' those dreams. And then, around noon, after I returned from my walk, I remembered the dream, because it included a woman who was Chinese. A group of us were going to have Chinese food at a restaurant that we all know, as we used to have Chinese food there, three times a week. But on this particular afternoon, we were walking, and we come to this fork in the road, and . . ."

"*Fork!* That's a very significant word in the realm of dreams. Remember *fork*! But go on."

". . . and for some reason the group got divided, and four of them were separated and went one way, and I was left with this Chinese woman. We had to go another way, but it wasn't anything, because at the bottom of the fork in the road, we could join-up with the bigger group; and I can't remember if in the dream I was talking to the Chinese woman, if I knew her, or not, or if I was just walking beside her. But then, I found myself alone, separated from this Chinese woman, walking this road on the left-hand side of the fork and, sudden-so, I am alone. There is no Chinese woman. I look down the road and see three men talking by the side of the road, and beside them, close-enough that they could touch it, was this small cow, a calf which I knew was a cow and not a bull, because it had no horns, and . . ."

"Goddamn! This is a *serious* dream! Note the word *horns*! Now, we have *fork* and *horn*. You know what that means, don't you? *To horn*, man! *To horn* a man. Eye-talians would kill a man for that. In the olden days you would challenge a man to a duel, if he *horned* you! Make him choose his weapon. Point o' honour. You were dreaming about *horning*, man! You were seeing your life before you, in terms of honour, and in the shape of a dream dealing with *horning*, and *forks*. Infidelity and betrayal. Honour. In plain words, your Chinese woman *was giving-'way the pussy behind your back*! Goddamn! Is this the Chinese woman in the snapshot? You should kill the bastard! *And* the three men? You ever know who these three bastards were?"

"No, man. No, it is not like that."

"Men always say, 'No, man, it isn't like that.'"

"This is a dream. It has nothing to do with sexual infidelity."

"You tell *me*! You said *horns*. Your word. Not mine! Let me tell you something. It is my profession. As a therapist, I know a dream is a funny thing. A dream deals not only with the present, or with the past. But more important than that, a dream tells you your future. Even if your future in the dream is not your future in real life, and is mistaken for the past. The Chinese woman could be dead in real life, but this is a dream. A dream is much more real than real life. You see what I'm saying? A dream is introspective, and it can tell you things before they happen, and it tells you things that happen even before you were born. But I am listening to you. Forget, if you want to, what I said about *horn* and *horning*."

"There were three men. They were standing and talking, and behind them was this cow with no horns, that's how I knew it was a cow; and I saw them continuing to talk and not paying attention to the cow, and I went my way with the Chinese woman beside me, feeling I was out of danger. And *then*, all of a sudden, the cow which was a calf turned into a bull with horns. And it came roaring at me. Its horns getting longer and longer, with froth at both sides of its mouth, and its eyes were red and big and bulging, and . . . the Chinese woman had disappeared from the dream . . ."

"Goddamn!"

". . . when I knew for certain it was coming straight at me, and when all I could see was the two horns, and that it was a bull, and as I said, the Chinese woman was no longer walking beside me, and all I could see were the two long horns, and the eyes pointing at me, and when I was sure, for certain, that the bull was coming at me, to gore me, or to kill me, I raised-up, I put-up my two hands, just-so! Look! Like this. And I *flinged* my two hands out in front of me, to protect me from getting pierced by the horns of the bull, and in so doing, with the flinging-out of my two hands, I lost my balance, and when I heard the shout '*Brugga-down-down!*' I fell outta the bed. And I am flat on my arse, on the floor!"

"You fall-outta bed?"

"*Brugga-down!*"

"Outta the bed?"

"Outta the fucking bed, like a motherfucker, *flat on my arse* – as you would say."

"You coulda-kill yourself."

"The noise woke-me-up."

"You take a serious fall, brother! Klein had such a fall offa the ladder."

"The first thing I did was to feel my head. And then my forehead, to see if I had-really fallen and hurt myself, or if I was still in the dream, and . . ."

"You had-fall, brother. You had-taken a fall, running away from the *horns* and the *horn*-ing, brother! Goddamn!"

". . . and when I touched my forehead I realized I was cut, and the blood was spurting outta my forehead."

"Blood?"

"Blood. And when I realize that I was cut, I *get-back-into* the bed, and fall *again*, a second time, now that I was awake. To see if I had-made a noise enough to wake up the neighbours on the left."

"What kind of a bed you coulda've fallen-out of? A bed has a certain height. So what kind of bed you screws on?"

"This is no laughing matter. I fell outta the blasted bed, and cut my forehead. Look! Right there. Just above my eyebrows, on the left, you can still see something like a bruise. The scar it left may be the same colour as my skin."

"Goddamn! You really *fall*!"

"But I didn't have the nerve to get-back-into the bed, and fall for real, just to test the noise I had-made when I fell in the dream. Ever since that night, I have been trying to find the meaning to this fall."

"You need not look any further. You *know* the meaning. I told it to you."

"And another thing. In the dream, I never found the group I was with. I never found the woman. I didn't go for Chinese food. So, I put some Limacol on my forehead, to stop the bleeding, and . . ."

"I gave you the meaning. I do this kind o' thing all the time, in my profession. There is only *two* factors you should be interested in. Number one, *horn*, or *horning*. Number two, the *number* of men. Namely three. You was being horned by three men, brother! It happens. It happens to the best of us! We are men, who think we're motherfuckers. It is usually we-kind o' men who gets horned most often. And not only by three men! We gets horned and horned and horned and horned. Take your licks. Take your medicine, brother. Join the fucking club! But you got me interested that a man your age is still carry-on with this business. What kind o' women you like?"

"What kind o' question is that?"

"There you go! I axe you a simple question, what kind o' women do you like to foop. And you answer my question with another question. That's a *sure* sign! The question frightens you. And your answer frightens you even more, because you can't lie, and you have to confess it. That's a *sure* sign. What kind o' women you like? If you're uncomfortable, you don't have to answer, so I can axe the question another way. Do you like women who are short? Do you like women who are fat? Who are tall? Who have big bubbies? Who have little bubbies? Whose chests are flat? Athletic women? Middle-age women? Rich women? Poor women? Independent-minded women? European women? African women? Wessindian women? White women? Black women? Blue women? Red women? Brown women? Two-tone women? Outta that *list*, pick out one! Is a simple question. What kind o' woman do you like?"

"What kind o' question is that?"

"A simple question."

"You're trying to analyze me."

"Okay. Short women?"

"No."

"Fat?"

"No."

"Tall?"

"No."

"With big, nice breasts?"

"No."

"Small breasts?"

"No."

"Women with flat chests?"

"No."

"Jesus Christ! What kind o' woman do you like, then? Goddamn! Do you like women, at all?"

"Not the ones you listed."

"Okay, you tell me, then. Athletic women? Women who wear jogging suits and those tight-fitting black outfits that runners wear, cyclist's pants?"

"No."

"Middle-age women?"

"Are you analyzing me?"

"I'm axe-ing you a goddamn simple question, brother. Like, what kind o' woman do you like to screw? Men do it. Women, too. A simple question. A question that was first axed in the Garden o' Eden. A question put to that stupid bastard, Adam, when Adam couldn't make up his goddamn mind to take a piece offa Eve, or take a bite outta the apple, speaking metaphorically, of course! If the Bible could talk about fooping, and try to hide it from people, but not from me, a big able man like me, and still think I am going to believe all that shit about an apple, when I know full-well that the reference is to pussy, plain and simple . . ."

"No!"

"You don't have to shout."

"No." I say this more softly, after I see a woman raise her eyes.

"So, you don't like middle-age women! What about rich women, women with bread?"

"Too high a price to pay."

"Poor women?"

"No."

"Independent-minded women?"

"Too independent."

"Are you a chauvinist?"

"Just a man who is looking for the right woman. No."

"What about a nice European woman?"

"Makes no difference to me."

"I could put you on to one o' my ex-wives."

"No *parlez-vous* women, please!"

"African?"

"Never met one."

"Never met one? Or never had one? You should try going-back-home, brother! Try-out your roots, if you see what I'm saying."

"No."

"I'm not talking about African Canadians or African Americans. I mean the real African woman. The real McCoy!"

"Six o' one and half-dozen of the other!"

"You're in deep trouble, brother. In deep shit! Try the Wessindian woman, then."

"No. No no no no no!"

"Five-times, no?"

"No."

"White women?"

"Makes no difference to me."

"Black women?"

"Makes no difference to me."

"But these things *have* to make a difference to a man. These things are important. Particularly as you live abroad, in a foreign country."

"Makes no fucking difference to me!"

"With pun intended, or not intended?"

"Pun, or no fucking pun, makes no difference to me. And you're getting me vexed, now."

"Blue women?"

"You mean women who have the blues? A woman who is depressed all the time, or a woman who is not happy, a woman . . . I'm sorry. I didn't mean to be . . ."

"Evasive. You're goddamn evasive. By the manner of your saying all these no's, I already got your answer, you bastard! This happens as the result of living alone, or by yourself, all these years. So, there's no point axeing you about a red woman, or a brown woman. You don't seem to like women."

"I don't like men, either."

"You are laying-down in bed one o' these nights, especially late at night, like round two o'clock in the morning. And you wish you had someone beside you. Someone, *anyone*, beside you. And you push-out your hand, outta custom, to touch that body, that lovely warm body. Because you must have had a body beside you *once*. So, you had a body beside you once, and you miss that body, miss the warmth if nothing else, just keeping you warm in these blasted North Amurcan winters that are so cold. And you wish-back to when you were younger. Thirty-five, thirty-nine, or even forty-nine perhaps. And you wish your life had-taken another path and you have a woman beside you; and having reach your age, fifty, sixty, seventy? You wish you were still young, a younger man with more punch, vim and vigour, and that you could handle something round twenty-one years of age, and even check out certain things that they say make a man *young*? When I say young, I don't mean age. I mean vim-and-vigour. Don't you have any o' these fantasies? Or wishes or dreams that don't involve falling and that contain horns and cows? Don't you ever dream of pussy? What you had? What you didn't *had*? Missed-opportunities? Put on your three-piece suit. Leave your wood-ants behind, and walk-out into the sunlight, brother! Walk-out into your favourite Yonge Street sunlight from the Lake right-back-up to your house. And as you walk, admire the chicks! Don't cost nothing. Don't *cause* nothing, either! And it's more better than playing with yourself. But you won't do this. So, you would put on your three-piece suit and leave the goddamn wood-ants and walk the streets from the Lake right-back-up to your house, and do *nothing* else?"

"What is interesting about this conversation . . ."

"You're talking like an essay, an academic paper, not like a *man*!"

"What is so interesting about this conversation, do you realize why this conversation is so interesting? I think that you and me are trying to answer questions which we would have asked each other if we had both remained in the same place. And if we had-lived in the same place, and seeing each other every day, some o' these questions we are now asking, we would know without asking them. It is like living alone, as you said. I don't mean not having a woman, or having a family. I mean living alone without anything like an anchor to tie-you-down, or anchor-you-back to your real first living. With no friends you grew up with, only strangers, people you meet after you come here, strangers who, because of something in this place and in this time, turn into friends. But not the real friends you grew up with, in the island."

"You're talking like a goddamn textbook!"

"You are asking a lotta questions, but they are questions I can't answer. There are questions that can only be answered in an island. Or like Klein, questions that can be answered only in a room with books. They are questions I already answer when I am sitting down in a chair, and, as you said, putting people, real people from my imagination, in the other chairs in the same room, and talking to them like Klein talks to his books. This is not the same thing as talking to yourself. But in a way, it is the same thing. Certainly, it is safer. I have asked myself all these questions already that you are asking me now. And when I ask myself these questions,

I can give any answer I wish, because nobody can hear my answers, or question me about my answers, or laugh at my answers, or disagree with them. I know what it means not to have somebody to talk with, or somebody to lie down beside; and I know what it is to be always walking the street out there on Yonge, and to see people and things and have to ask yourself the question, and have to answer-back yourself. As the song says, about walking along lonely streets, watching people passing by and not seeing you, even though you raise a gesturing hand; but nothing happens. This happens to old people when they get old in a city that is young like this city. And suppose I ask the wrong question? Suppose I ask the *right* question? Suppose the wrong woman smiled? You give yourself the *wrong* answer. If you and me had-come to this country together, all these questions you're asking me, you wouldn't have to ask me. You would know the answers. And I would know the answers. It is the time that separates me and you, that has us now, in this concentrated time, pressed against the two walls of our experience."

"What kind o' shite are you talking to me? What kind o' textbook bullshit is this? What kind o' bed was it, if I might axe you a normal question? What kind o' bed it was?"

"It is like a big piece of something, guts or spirit, is taken out of my body, something like a heart, my heart. But the only difference is that if it is a piece, even just a little piece of my heart, I wouldn't be here with you now, in this bar talking this way. The bed you asked me about?"

"What kind o' bed you goddamn fall-out-of?"

"Just a bed. An ordinary bed. You could buy one at any store. But my bed has an iron spring. I had a friend once, a woman, who had to move in a hurry. One Friday night, she had planned to slip through the second-floor window with her bags, before the land-lord came home, and jump onto the roof of the garage, and then onto the ground to escape, without paying the rent; and as the iron bedstead with the iron springs couldn't fit into her bags or through the window, she left it for me to keep for her, until she found a place, or found the rent. She hasn't told me if she found a place so far; so I'm still keeping it for her. I sleep on an iron bedstead owned by an escaped tenant, you might call it that. So, with a normal mat-tress and a normal box spring, plus the iron bedstead, I now have a bed that is abnormally high, that reaches me almost to my hips, or my waist . . ."

"How tall are you, now?"

"Five-eleven and a half. Or six."

"Then the bed is three, three-and-a-half, four!"

"So, until I can give-her-back the iron bedstead with the iron springs, I have to keep it and sleep in it, even if I fall out of it again, as it is so high off the floor. But I am telling you about a need. That is what I am really telling you. About a need. I have a need. But I don't really know what the need is."

"You don't have no goddamn need! What need? All you need is a woman. A woman to give you a good, regular foop, even if it is only once a month! Even if you can't really foop, or foop-her-back! Goddamn, it's my profession to know these things and deal with these things, and tell people the plain truth about these things. And you're talking like a goddamn North Amurcan, with your goddamn *needs*. You are not talking like a Wessindian. *Your* needs, goddammit? You ain't have no needs, no more needs than the next person, than any one o' these bastards in this bar with us, no more than anybody else! Need is not your problem. Your goddamn problem is sexual deprivation, or sexual loneliness, if you see what I'm saying. And in your case, I will break my cardinal rule when I am giving people advice and therapy and professional advice, and say this. I will break all my rules, and say to you: a man suffering from sexual and sociological loneliness . . . that in your case . . . your problem is not a simple case of just needing a woman. Listen to my words. All. You. Need. Is. Companionship. Since you have no sexual drive, and you can't foop. You understand me? All. You. Goddamn need. Is. Female companionship. A foopless relationship. One that don't include sex. But have you ever thought of a dog? Or a cat? Or a durabel? You know what those are? You sure-as-hell can't call wood-ants companions, or pets! You don't kill pets with cans o' Black Flag! So, it makes more sense to me for you to talk to a goddamn dog, and I hate the bastards, than to be killing ants whiching you can't talk to. And then to start dreaming and falling-out of a goddamn bed that you're keeping for some hippie-woman who skipped town without paying her rent! Did you have an affair with this woman? In my professional opinion, you *did*. At least, *could*. Hence the dream with the *horns* and *horning* in it; and then falling-out of the goddamn bed owned by this woman. I am laughing. I can't help laughing. You never looked at it that way?"

"Once upon a time, there was a fellow I know, from Barbados; and this fellow had this woman, and he used to work in the States, and he would come home every-other Friday night by plane, from New York to Toronto International, and go straight from the airport down into the suburbs where the woman lived, up in Scarborough; and he would tell the woman when he was coming because he didn't want to have to pay all that money, travelling back and forth, and arrive and find out that she had gone out to a bingo game, or to a West Indian club like Cutty's Hideaway where they dance to calypso and reggae, and spend his money on plane fare for nothing, even though Cutty's Hideaway on Danforth Avenue is not so far from her place in Scarborough. So, he made it his practice to call her the day before he was to leave La Guardia and tell her the time his plane was arriving in Toronto; but he wasn't really putting her on her guard, or in case, or leaving himself open for a disappointment, because she lived with her mother, and she had a small son, who . . ."

"For him?"

"What you mean?"

"Did she have the goddamn child for the Barbadian man you're telling about?"

"No. Well, yes. No, and yes. She said the boy was his, but he didn't think it was his, after he added up the days and the nights and the times, and when she became pregnant and told him she was carrying the child. But he liked the boy, and supported him. He always brought a gift for her and the boy, chocolates, a stuffed animal, a ladies' nail-file case and a bottle of brandy for the grandmother. So, on this particular night, it was minus thirty-five, and he arrived with his bags, three bags, even though he was only spending two nights out of the weekend, a leather briefcase, a leather suit-bag, and a leather duffel-type . . ."

"He liked *leather!*"

". . . and he remembered putting the bags in the trunk of the taxi and when he took them out to carry them into the lobby of the apartment, they were so much heavier; but he remembered putting the bags down in the lobby of the apartment building, in the small lobby you come to just before you actually enter the building itself. He rang the buzzer on the panel just above a radiator, because they had radiators in those days, and he rings and rings and no answer, and he rings again, but the plane had-arrived at nine-thirty from La Guardia, earlier than it was due to arrive, and it took him a half-hour to come from the airport to

Scarborough in all that snow, to the apartment in the taxi, so he rang but he didn't think anything of it. But he still rang the buzzer again, and all the time he is ringing the buzzer he is trying to remember if he is ringing the right number, because she had called him to say she was moving to a larger apartment in the same building, and he is wondering if the number he is ringing is the right number, not only to the apartment, but if he is at the right apartment building. So he takes up his three bags, getting heavier now through his disappointment and the cold in the outer lobby, and holding them and slipping on the ice and getting his trousers covered in the deep snow. He went to a pay-phone and checked the number and the address. He was ringing the right buzzer. So, he comes back to the lobby, and rang the number some more, but still there was no answer – this is after he had-tried the number on the telephone. All this time, in and out, are people coming and going. One time he sees the same three people. Two women and a man, who had come out and passed him hours ago, going back in, and he is still there ringing the buzzer, in the lobby, wearing a black winter coat, a three-piece suit, boots, and scarf, ringing the goddamn buzzer, as you would say. And then an idea strikes him. Supposing, he says to himself, she isn't home? Supposing she has moved? People, especially West Indians, can pick themselves up and move suddenly, for no reason. Supposing she is in Guyana, and he has not remembered that she called him and told him she was going to Guyana to visit her sisters and her aunt. 'Cause remember, her mother lives with her and her son, in the apartment. And she may need a vacation. And this fellow with the three heavy bags is supposing and supposing and supposing. But his mind would not let him start supposing the obvious thing. His mind is only coming so close to it, and then shying away from the real supposing. So he hit on an idea. Another idea. He studied the panel of buzzers, checking the names he does not know, even including hers. She never put her real name on the panel. He checks the panel of buzzers with the names beside them, looking for the number to the superintendent's apartment. When he rings the buzzer to the superintendent's apartment, a recording comes on. '*The superintendent of this building is on duty between the hours of seven and ten on Mondays, Tuesdays, Wednesdays, and Thursdays. On Fridays, the superintendent is off-duty at eight. For emergencies, call the police.*' It is midnight, or later. The superintendent is off-duty, and the man is standing-up in the outer lobby where there is no heat, tired as a horse, with his ears plugged-up from the flying, and ringing the buzzer and the woman won't answer . . ."

"The super is a mother!" John says.

". . . and another idea hits him. He realized in the heat of the moment, in the heat of the situation, like when you are angry or quarrelling with a woman and you want to say something in your defence, but you are

117

so vexed that you can't remember the words you want to say, or should say, to end the quarrel and defend yourself. Or like when somebody calls you a nigger, and you know before he even calls you so that you have practised a response that is more hurtful, that has to be more hurtful than that, but when the name cuts into your heart, the wound is so deep and so sharp and there is so much blood pouring out of it, that you forget in the moment of the cut to say what you had practised you would say. Only after the quarrel or the assault of that word is over and fades away a little, or the fight is over, *bram!* that word, or the response to *that* other word comes back to you. He has an idea. He has this idea. Ring *any* buzzer. If it answers, it will release the lock on the outside entrance door. But this Barbadian fellow feels so stupid and humiliated that now, after twelve o'clock at night, on a Friday night in the suburbs, he is ringing a buzzer, ringing a buzzer, ringing a buzzer . . ."

"If the motherfucker had-ring that buzzer in Brooklyn, *on any street* in Brooklyn – Nostrand, Schenectady, Fulton – any of them, even in a black neighbourhood, from nine-something in the night till after twelve midnight, his ass woulda-been *shot!* Out goes you, Jack!"

"He has this next idea to ring the buzzer beside the name of any woman on the panel. And she answers, 'Who is it?', and the fellow says, 'John,' and the voice coming back at him through the panel and the intercom says, 'Come in, Johnnie!' and the door flies open, and he plants his winter boot between the door, and *ease-in* the three bags, and immediately he feels the warmness in the main lobby. And his body is so tired and he remembers how long he was ringing the buzzer that he almost collapses in the fresh warmness. So he remains standing for a moment feeling the warmness of the lobby bathe his skin, and for a moment he forgets completely he is calling the woman on the thirty-third floor, the woman he has come to see. All he wants now is the warmness of the lobby, to sit down and rest, and get off his feet. Or just lie down on the couch in the main lobby, or in a bed, and go fast to sleep, and forget the woman. But just as he imagined how warm it would be in a bed, he remembered her again. And then, he has to place his winter boot in the elevator to prevent the door from closing and the elevator going back up without him. He eases his three bags in the elevator, and as he does so he forgets to press number 33 on the elevator panel. Not that he really forgot to press 33, it was more like he was scared, thinking what was going to happen when the elevator reached the thirty-third floor, and he had to get off, and walk along the hallway with its red carpet with red patterns like vases – you remember Roman vases, or urns, *Grecian urns?* There are Grecian urns in the pattern of the red carpet that runs all the way from one end of the hallway to the next, by the fire-escape door with a big red EXIT above it, a distance of about one hundred yards, a good hundred-yard dash."

"'Ode on a Grecian Urn.' By Keats."

"Wordsworth."

"Keats."

"Wordsworth!"

"Keats! *Thou still unravish'd bride of quietness, / Thou foster-child of silence and slow time, / Sylvan historian, who canst thus express / a flowery tale more sweetly than our rhyme* . . .' You think Wordsworth could write poetry like *this*? Is Keats! Don't you remember we did this poem in our School Certificate from Cambridge University?"

"I remember the poem, too, man! But I tell you it is Wordsworth. *'What men or gods are these? What maidens loth? / What mad pursuit? What struggle to escape? / What pipes and timbrels? What wild ecstasy?'* . . . *'What wild ecstasy?'* . . . Wordsworth!"

"Keats's hand is written all-over that poem, man! You can smell Keats's sweat and perspiration pouring-down from this poem!"

"Who in this bar would know? Let's axe the barman." And he beckons the barman over. "Buddy, right? I hear the patrons call you so. It's Buddy?" John says.

"Buddy," Buddy says. So John asks him, and the barman shrugs his shoulder, and says he has never heard of Keats or Wordsworth, but he knows a fellow who comes in here who says he writes poetry, a Canadian fellow. But he likes Grecian urns, he says.

"I worked for fifteen years for a Greek fellow who owns a Greek restaurant," he tells us, "and on the menu and on the interior design, like on the doors and the window panes and the matches, was all these things like urns. I asked the owner, my boss, one day what these things is, and he says to me, 'Grecian urns, Buddy, Grecian urns. Arts from my country.' I love those urns."

"Well, never mind. Give us two more double martinis. The same as before."

"Coming right up, gentlemen," Buddy says, grinning and laughing. We have made a friend.

"One hundred yards of red carpet with red Grecian urns that he walks along, not making any noise although the three heavy bags seem as if they have dead bodies in them, not knowing what is going to happen when he knocks on the door of the woman's apartment . . . and he is thinking of the time when he was a runner at elementary school and at the Combermere School for Boys, when this same distance travelled over by him so many times got longer and more painful with each sprint, longer than one hundred yards. More than this fear of the interminable nature of the hallway was the deeper fear that he would not reach the tape, and that he would not ever again reach the tape first. There is fear as he travels over one hundred yards of red Grecian urns that he knows so well, and that has brought him such victory and such pleasure of satisfaction. The Grecian urns in the pattern of the red carpet are like his own trophies of cheap silver, metal painted to look like silver. The urns multiply with the distance and go out of focus, as he wonders what reception he is going to get when he reaches her apartment, just as he always wondered what reception he would get if he reached the tape, and was not the first to break it. He walks up to the door and stands outside it for a few minutes, listening to the noise inside, imagining what noise is inside, what is going to happen to that noise he imagines he hears when he presses the bell, what dream she is coming out of, what dream her son is in, and will he scream at the shrill ringing of the bell repeating its sound in the dark insides of the bedroom, and interrupt his nightmare? Will her mother be the one to come to the door, armed with a kitchen knife, as she does when she answers the door after dusk back home in Georgetown in Guyana where she says that 'all those bastards want to do is choke-and-rob we.' She was robbed on her last visit by a man who held a cutlass to her throat. He imagines the woman in her soft blue nightgown that is not real silk, not the pure silk she is accustomed to at cheaper prices in her native Guyana, but which fits her like a priceless outer skin of silk, and riding her body like kisses over her hips and breasts as she moves about the bedroom, rubbing the rheum out of her eyes and looking more seductive in her drowsiness. Her eyes are larger than in the daytime, and her lips, always large and now more luscious and quivering with desire in the night time. And he rang the bell. And froze. And waited for the door to be flung open and for him to face the glistening blade of the seven-inch kitchen knife he had seen her mother use to snap the head off a red snapper, or make mince with a shoulder of pork for the making of garlic-pork, which he ate with them the three Christmas mornings, before the boy was born. The hallway becomes quiet, quiet. In the quietness he can hear the waves in the sea at Paynes Bay, and he can hear the first sound of the conch-shell announcing the arrival of the fishing boats, and he can hear the pop of the starter's gun at the beginning of the hundred-yard dash, and he can hear the rattling of knives and forks in the drawer in the kitchen, and the rustling of the nightgowns worn to bed at night. The stillness is making him guilty, his deliberate breaking of the peace within the sweet-smelling apartment where she burns incense from India for the sake of its fragrance and its acridness which kills the smell of raw red snapper and curry. No one comes to the door. He rings the bell again. He can hear it from where he is standing. No one moves inside the apartment. But the stillness of the night makes the hallway become dark, although it is bathed in fluorescent light, for the entire one hundred yards of its distance. But he is standing in the dark and is becoming aware of things that come at you at night out of the darkness. A head of a woman peeped out of an apartment, and said nothing, and withdrew without expressing disgust. He cannot remember if he knows this neighbour from his previous visits. Perhaps, and knows that the neighbour's lips are sealed against disclosure of her personal knowledge of things. And on his other side, a body comes out into the middle of the hallway, and he can see the outline of her legs through the penetrating fluorescent light which rips the thin nightdress, the waist down to her feet. She says nothing and just stands and stares. He thinks he sees a smile on her face. Not a smile of recognition only, but also a smile that contains information she is not willing to divulge at this ungodly hour of the night. And fearing that more heads and bodies will come out in punctuation of his pressing the bell, he takes up his three leather bags, and moves the short distance to the elevator. He presses the buzzer for the carriage to come and carry him from these neighbourly eyes. Just before the elevator comes, he goes back one last trembling time to the apartment door and presses his right ear against the dark-stained plywood, and hears movement inside and a swishing of cloth, and a rattling of knives and forks in the drawer beside the refrigerator. But it is the noise from the elevator coming up to rest beside him, and open its mouth, and take him in. And down, down, down he goes in his retreat, wishing he was a braver man, wishing he was a man who didn't care about scenes and neighbours in nightgowns looking out; wishing he was a strong man, brave enough to shout out the name of this sleeping woman, and have the sleeping neighbours open their doors to welcome him, or laugh at him; wishing that he was brave enough to kick the door in, and bring scandal and attention to all of them; wishing that he didn't care how brutal the Toronto cops are to men stalking and beating, assaulting and harassing women; wishing that he could face the cops and face his reputation put upon the front pages of the *Toronto Star* and the *Toronto Sun*, in the large, full proof of print. He would disregard the papers heralding the image and the stereotyping of his West Indian race and colour. But he is a coward. A stupid fucking goddamn Barbadian black coward! Down, down, down in the elevator, which is hot, hotter than the lobby after the cold, damp, small vestibule where the panel of buzzers and names are installed; down, down, down he goes, and gets out of the elevator and sits in the lobby, and watches the colour of the thick glass on the front door change, until he can see the outline of trees and cars and people moving, and buses driving by, and more people coming out of the four elevators behind him, on their way to work and on their way after a night of playing dominoes, and a night spent with women. 'Morning,' a woman greets him. 'Cold again, today, eh?' a woman says, as she pulls her scarf in a tighter fit, as she grabs the front of her winter coat. And her coat grabbed in this fashion makes her body warm, and makes her body look smaller. 'Boy, *what* we doing in this damn place, eh? You have a good day, son.' A man comes out, and looks at him and moves to the door; and before he places his hand on the horizontal metal bar to let himself out into the cold morning, he looks back a second time, and says something with the movement of his body and his eyes; and the man sitting on the bracket of the radiator realizes that he has seen this same man three times in the hours he has spent tracking the woman down and ringing the bell, from the time he first stood in the small outer lobby, ringing the buzzer. The man is Indian. From the West Indies. Younger than he. In the new dawn of morning, a taxi drives up to the front door, and he rushes to the door, and beckons to the driver. A passenger gets out; the driver nods his head, and tells him to come. The man in the lobby helps him with the three leather bags, and before he closes the door behind him, the man says, 'Rass! What a night, eh, bwoy!' The tires of the taxi scratch the ice on the driveway, skid a little, and it moves out into the Saturday-morning traffic, going west. He thinks of crabs moving over the beach. 'Where to this time?' The airport, he tells the driver. 'Had a good night?' The radio receiver in the taxi is loud, barking names and addresses and warnings, not intended for this driver, and which he listens to nevertheless, but does not answer."

"Goddamn!" John says. "This is the first time I have heard you talk like this! Goddamn! Normally, not even in my profession, do I hear a man bear his soul like this."

"It wasn't *me* I was talking about."

"Bullshit! You were a sprinter!"

"This story is not my story."

"Getouttahere! You came second in the hundred-yard sprint at school!"

"It isn't. If it was, I would-have told it in the first person."

"Are you for real? Come on! You're talking to me, your ace-boon, remember? The fellow who grew up with you, who went with you to the Public Library every Saturday. Look. Lemme tell you something. Women can face the truth easier than men, and are the only people who can face the truth the way you just faced it, though you're trying to bullshit me that this isn't you. Your language, man. Your language gave-you-way. The emotion in your story, even the details of the story, the hundred-yard dash reference; and even if the details of the story don't all apply to you, the language in the narrative is yours, brother. The language. Plus, there is certain details that only the perpetrator, or the participant, or a man who experienced that experience could know. But who the fuck cares? Who cares? There ain't one man, not one motherfucker who hasn't been fucked-over by a woman, whether he deserve it or not. And most men, lemme tell ya, fellow, most men deserve to be fucked! So, you were *horned*. Fuck it! You was had, baby, *you was had*! I told you so, hours ago, before we had this last martini. I told you the meaning of the dream about falling outta bed and about the bull with the horns and the three men. Surprising, maybe for you, but not really surprising to me. You went over the *same* things in your dream as in your story. You was *had*. But you can't face it, even though you know, *ipso-factually* speaking, you was had. Horned. Cuckold. Cudgelled. Call it what the fuck you like, *you was fucked*, baby! Join the club."

He is looking at me, like a brother, a big brother who cannot feel the actual pain but whose compassion is meant to ease it. And although I do not have a brother, John is always like one to me, a big brother. So, here he is now, sitting in this crowded bar, in this foreign city, Toronto, so far from Durham, North Carolina, in the South where he now lives, giving me the feeling that he has been coming to this bar for years, every afternoon, with me, and listening to my stories, and understanding them. As if the cord that first joined us from those days on the beach at Paynes Bay, with the sand the same colour as the conch-shell, has never been severed.

"Enter the brotherhood, baby. Another?"

"Sure!"

"Change the gin, this time."

"Bombay gin," I suggest.

"You-got-it!"

"I never told this to anyone," I say.

"You think you had me fooled, eh?" he says. "Open your heart, man."

"You know something? Do you know that I have never in my life made a choice? A choice that was my own choice. Beginning with the place I went to school, Trinity College here. Do you know I have never made a choice, I mean, never did anything I *knew* was what I wanted to do, by my own decision, and not what either somebody-else, or the system, made me do. Am I making sense? I have never had the opportunity to talk about this. Forty, forty-five, fifty years I held this inside myself. But when I think about it, I know in my mind that this is the meaning of the experience of living in a place you are not born in. And you know something else? Women. I have never made a personal choice, meaning I never found myself in the position to pick out the woman who is a woman I want and love, *my choice.* What I mean by this is that it is either the situation, the circumstance, like standing at a bus stop, or in an art gallery looking at pictures which I don't understand, and a person, a woman comes behind me and she then stands beside me, and begins to say something, and we talk, and then I would invite her for a coffee or a drink, purely out of boredom, and one thing would lead to another. And before you hear the shout, something is started. But it is not my choice to have something started. Only the coffee or the drink. Am I making sense to you? Am I the only man with this vacantness, this vacuum of making choices? This makes any sense to you? For instance, living here in this city. Toronto. You're surrounded with a majority of women who come from a different culture and background than you. Women you meet but do not know. Even with the rise in immigration and multiculturalism, still you are surrounded by strangers. In your job.

On the street. In classes. In bed. At a concert. At an art gallery. And at a bus stop. Everywhere. But deep down in your heart, you're fighting it and fighting it. And you know something? It's a losing battle. Looking for that special woman you really want to know, or that *other* woman. In your social group, in your work, in your mind. As things, as these things work on your mind, you're still walking around like a zombie, with your body telling you one thing, and your heart telling you something else. And I find myself painting women black. In colour. And in culture. Not jet-black, but black when they are not, and I am colouring them black. You know what I mean? The loveliest white woman, bright, decent, intelligent, with a good body and character. Just saying these things, I hope nobody is hearing me say them, because I am telling you things that I tell myself, in the privacy of my house, sitting down alone, with the goddamn jumbo can of Black Flag in my hand. And for somebody-else but you to hear these thoughts, they would certainly certify me as mad. *Worse!* A racist. Am I a racist?"

"Cobblers are black. The ants you kill with your Black Flag are black."

"Am I a racist?"

"You're goddamn, a goddamn lonely man."

"Am I?"

"Cobblers and wood-ants are black."

"What does that mean?"

"Nothing. It don't mean shit!"

"Cobblers are black and ants are black? It must mean something in your profession."

"Women are more honest than men in relationships."

"Women are more honest in relationships?"

"Not that I am a sex therapist. I won't touch that with a ten-foot pole. But I happen to know a few things. I see it in them, all the time. Honesty. I'm not talking about fidelity, although you may have a point there. Women are more honest in relationships. It sounds like one of the Ten Commandments, doesn't it?"

"I remember once-upon-a-time, that . . ."

"Not again! Goddamn!"

"It was me. I was the person."

"Who was you?"

"The man in the lobby. The man in the story. The man going-up in the elevator, and ringing the apartment bell. The man going-down in the elevator. The man is me."

"Who was the Indian?"

"I remember, once-upon-a-time, when I was at the apartment, she was cooking cow-heel with curry, red kidney beans and rice, and it was strange because I had never seen anybody cook a cow-heel. And an Indian fellow was there. Her mother called him 'Cousin Cyril,' and then *she* called him 'Cousin Cyril.' And then the little boy, who was just learning to talk, called him 'Douzen Cyllil.'"

"There you go again, with the same cow-thing. Cow? Cow-heel? Cow-horn? Horn? *Horning?* Follow your instincts, man. Always try not to disbelieve your instincts because you happen to live in a so-called sophisticated society that is civilize. We are instincts-men. We live by our instincts. Cow-heel and cow-horns. *Horning*!"

"Sitting down here this afternoon, or this evening, whichever it is now, reminds me when we used to sit-down on the beach after school, after elementary school, and after Combermere, and then later on, after Harrison College, and talk, in our cut-down trousers with the sandflies coming into our mouths and biting us, and we couldn't even see them. Or watching the crabs crawling over the sand making noise and scratching little trails back into the sea, and how the sea would take them up and swallow them, and erase the trails. And in all that time, in all those times sitting on the beach, I never knew if those crabs could swim."

"I know *you* can't. But crabs can swim."

"Once-upon-a-time, I was going to learn to swim. After I came here. It was a Canadian woman who was at Trinity with me who threatened to teach me to swim, in a swimming pool, in a public swimming pool, not in the sea. Or the Lake. But that was back in 1959 or 1960, when swimming pools in this city were restricted to white people, and black people couldn't get a dip in them. Matter of fact, there is a lotta things I never had the urge to do, in this place and in this country. The man serving us, the barman, for instance. For years and years you would never see a black man as a waiter in a bar in this city, farthermore a barman, a bartender in a bar that was . . ."

"The son of a bitch still don't know Keats or Wordsworth! But he sure knows his Grecian urns!"

"As if the colour of our skin was going to rub-off in the water and turn the water blackish. In 1959, I could not enter a public swimming pool and take a dip. A public swimming pool! They didn't have signs saying 'No Blacks Allowed nor Dogs' when the woman was trying to get me to learn to swim. They were already taken down. But they used to have them. The restriction was written in actions and attitudes. In people's minds. Once, though, a fellow from Grenada jumped in a pool, and the moment the splash settled, everybody was outta that pool. He wondered what happened. Nobody told him what happened. Not a thing. The only person who remained in the pool was his friend who had taken him to the pool in the first place, Max Goldstein. Max Goldstein didn't tell him nothing, for years; but years later when the two of them were lawyers practising on Bay Street, which in Toronto is the same as Wall Street in the States, Max and him were having a drink in a bar much like this one, and Max said, 'Fuck it! Something I had to tell you years ago when the two of us were in final year. Remember the pool I took you to on Eglinton Avenue West? It was the summer. In July. Fucking hot that afternoon. Remember? And you did a back-flip in the fucking pool? The next day, my father got a fucking letter from the fucking superintendent. Friend, you don't know the time it took me to say this. You muddied their fucking pool with that back-flip! Fuck it! How many years since we were called to the bar? Five? Five and one spent in fucking Articling, two in Law School. Five and five're ten. Plus one. Eleven. Plus two is thirteen. Thirteen fucking years it's taken me to tell you this. To admit this fuckery! And here you are today, with your own fucking swimming pool in your backyard fucking bigger than that fucking community pool. Ain't life a fucker?' With me, it's the same thing with golf and tennis. Tennis and golf, two things I distinguish a man from the West Indies by. Meaning that if they come to Trinity College, and start a lotta talk about going on the golf-links or the tennis courts, I know they're full o' shit! That they weren't really black back in the West Indies! It used to be like that. Now, there is a change."

I sit and remember those early days and I try to forget the worst of them.

He sits and sips his drink.

"Your mother was a riot," he says at last. "Your mother was something else! You ran through my gate once, in the backyard one Friday evening after school, with your legs marked-up and your shirt tear-up, after your mother had-dropped some of the stiffest licks in your ass! Remember? You wanted to be like one o' those boys who were lay-by early from school, at two in the afternoon instead of three when school normally lay-by, so they could go down to the Garrison Savannah

Tennis Club and *feel* tennis balls. Remember? Perhaps *that* is why you don't like tennis. And after you left the island, and was here studying, it took a man like the Great Dipper Barrow, Errol Walton Barrow, when he became the first Prime Minister, that the first official thing he did was to check some musty files in the old Colonial Secretary's office, the Col-Sec office, and find out that the Garrison Savannah Tennis Club was a public facility, just like the public swimming pool you was talking about. The Savannah was renting the premises from the Guvvament for one dollar a year. *One dollar!* Goddamn! And your mother, just like my Old Lady, was a woman uneducated in a formal sense, but really educated better than us, in the real sense. My Old Lady . . ." He takes a large white handkerchief, folded into quarters, from the top pocket in his jacket, lets it fall to its full size, and wipes his eyes. When he takes the handkerchief opened with a slight fling of his hand, from his face, I can see that his eyes are filled with tears. "I didn't see her being lowered in the goddamn grave. I did not get the message in time to lift her goddamn head. My goddamn Old Lady, a *queen!*"

I keep my martini glass in my hand, without tasting the powerful, clear liquid in it, while he allows the tears to come into his eyes and fall into his glass and fall on his expensive custom-made suit. Some men close to us watch, and hold their heads down, sensing the moment of passion, knowing of some powerful emotion in their own lives, which was so full and uncontrollable that

135

they themselves had done this same thing in public. But shedding tears in a bar? And a man doing it? And not even sitting beside a woman, to make this expression more understandable, or rationalizing? Or as a camouflage?

"Only once before this, only once, have I done this in public. Cried like a goddamn baby. Couldn't help myself. Years ago. At a funeral. At Gloria's funeral. Gloria was a woman from Barbados who for some reason found herself in France when I was still married to Hyacinthe, my *parlez-vous* wife, and was a gradual-student. Met her at a Wessindian club where they played calypsos that were bad and old by the time they reached Paris-France. Looked good, too! Gloria was a big woman, with big eyes, with big legs, with big hips, with big bubbies, with a goddamn big heart. Had a man. Not a very good man. Would invite me and some other students to her apartment for real down-home cooking. Her favourite was cou-cou and tin-salmon, canned salmon. And coconut bread. You know, I would go to her apartment by bus and train, all hours of the night and in all kinds o' weather, and sometimes there would be the two of us. Just Gloria and me. And as I said, this woman with big hips and big bubbies and big eyes and lips was looking so good! And it never crossed my mind to axe her for a piece, although I *knew* that she woulda give me a piece, if I had-just axed, in the right way. With me and Gloria it was just a matter of companionship . . ."

"The companionship you were telling me to have with a woman?"

"That kind o' companionship."

"To me, that kind of companionship is reserved for a man and a woman who are old, and who have retired from fooping, so they hold hands in front of the television and chew their gums, or play patience. It is an honourable estate."

"But guess what happened?"

"Companionship, for me, is just before you die, and having a woman to check . . ."

"And later on, after years and years, guess what happened?"

"She offered you a piece!"

"It was one summer afternoon, and me and some other Wessindians was in her backyard, and we were playing dominoes and really having a good time now that summer was here at last, reminding us of back home, and drinking some rum that her mother had-send from Barbados. And the conversation turned to family and relatives and family trees; and how, back home, a man could be your family and drop dead and you would never know it until after he is six-feet-deep, dead as shite, because the place, the whole o' Barbados, is so incestuous and close-mouth about it. And Gloria start tracking-back her family, second-cousins to third-cousins and fourth-cousins, back back back, ripping-off the bark from the family tree, and Jesus Christ! Me and Gloria was related! Me and Gloria was first-cousins!

Can you imagine that? Can you imagine that if I had-axed Gloria for a piece that evening when I was in her apartment, what I woulda done? Just me and her. After eating and after I had doze-off and slept most of the night, I wake up the next morning and see Gloria there on the floor sleeping in a nightgown. I could see-through the nightgown that had a tear in it. Trans-parent as if she had just come-outta the sea. I was sleeping on her couch. 'Man, you does-snore like a blasted horse! *Two* horses!' is what Gloria tell me when she wake up. And she made breakfast. Three fried eggs each, six pieces o' bacon, toast, two thick slices o' coconut bread, and some of the roast-pork from the night before. The bacon was fried too hard, though. It was burnt. And as we're eating and talking and joking, and Gloria is sitting in front of me in her see-through nightgown . . . it was pink. Gloria liked pink. Anything pink. There's Gloria, sitting in front o' me in her night-gown, and one bubbie, her left breast, drooping-over the top. And I sitting down and watching that bubbie making little jumps whenever she move her arm to reach over for another strip o' over-fried bacon; or use a knife to cut-off a slice o' coconut bread. And I see that nipple get a little more black and start to look funny like how pores does-get bigger, and as if the pores where the milk comes out, or used to come out, for Gloria at this time was a woman who-stopped having thrildren . . . her two thrildren were already grown men . . . that bubbie start to get a little stiff. And

138

the black circle round it get blacker. And I could almost see the blood pumping into the veins in her bubbie. And all I did was to continue sitting and eating the three fried eggs and the eight pieces o' dried bacon. I had two of hers. And then, the moment she got up and went in the bathroom, the man who was her boyfriend arrive. And the three o' we played dominoes again, till past midnight. But suppose I had-axe Gloria for a piece? And you know something? I was much younger then, in my early-twenties, or late-twenties. I could not tell you, in sexual terms, what the thing with the pores in her bubbie was telling me! I did not know the meaning of it."

"What meaning? The nipples or the black circles round the bubbies?"

"The flesh was willing, man! The flesh was willing! But I did not have that knowledge."

"The spirit was willing."

"But the flesh was weak. Now, on another Saturday, she had-just called me, to invite me up to her new condominium, 'cause she had-made a hit offa a lottery ticket. *Millions o' francs she win,* and had-bought this condominium in the suburbs just outside o' Paris. Me and Hyacinthe was still living in a room in Paris. Gloria always said, 'Tummuch blasted Wessindians living now in Paris, and they malicious as shite and I don't want none o' those bastards to know my business!' So she moved to the suburbs just outside Paris, a lovely place with all the modern conveniencies, balcony, and a spare room for guesses, in a three-bedroom condominium. So she called me to invite me up to christen the place, 'cause she was cooking cou-cou and canned salmon the day. She called me at three o'clock the afternoon. The cou-cou was to be ready for five o'clock. I was still in my one-room apartment trying to do some work, with Hyacinthe in my ass, '*Beaucoup* years you graduate? I wait *longtemps* for you to graduate, *oui?*' when the telephone rang. 'Gloria dead,' the voice say. *Gloria dead?* 'She dead. She just dead.'"

He takes his handkerchief from his jacket pocket a second time. This time, there are no tears. He sticks the handkerchief, after folding it back into quarters, into his pocket again, leaving its four corners like church spires in full view in the pocket. "Gloria dead. The day after. I found out. She was turning the meal-corn to make the cou-cou when she dropped-fucking-dead! Don't you think that is a goddamn shame, a goddamn loss, a goddamn shock? So, now, I am at the funeral. At the service. In one of the biggest churches in Paris; and all the years that I know Gloria, I never heard Gloria talk nothing 'bout going to church, or talk nothing about church, although she knew *every* hymn in *Hymns Ancient & Modern,* by heart. And another thing I find out about Gloria, after she dead. Gloria had-paid for her grave and a tombstone five years before she really died. The things you learn afterwards about a person, no matter how close you is to that person in the flesh. But when the person dead, all these things you learn about the person, for the first time. Gloria had-buy a plot to bury herself in. Five years before! And whilst we would be slamming the doms on a Friday night, right into Saturday evening, we would be singing hymns, especially if a fellow or a girl was about to get beaten six-love; and it would be Gloria who knew the words, and the number of the hymn in the hymnbook. Gloria would sing the first four words in 'The Day Thou Gavest,' and *that* meant that somebody was in danger of getting a six-love in their ass . . ."

And we laugh. We can see the barman pouring a little extra gin in our martinis, and heading in our direction. And John, in a soft voice, still retaining a touch of the timbre and a trace of his training as a chorister in the Cathedral Church, begins to sing the hymn which to us back in the island is the hymn sung always at funerals . . . "*The day Thou gavest, Lord, is ended; The darkness falls at Thy behest; To Thee our morning hymns ascended, Their praise shall sanctify our rest.*"

"Hymn four-seventy-seven," I tell him.

"How many times you and me sang this hymn? In school, when there was nobody dead? In the choir at funerals, when we got two shillings for singing? At Services-of-Songs, when fishermen gather inside a rum-shop, or in somebody's front-house? On a Sunday? We sang almost *every* hymn in the hymnbook. And at the first sign o' trouble, my Old Lady and yours always sing this hymn . . . *The day Thou gavest, Lord* . . ."

"How many hymns are in the hymnbook? You ever counted them? How many you know?"

"Seven, eight hundred? And I'm *not* gonna axe the goddamn barman this time, neither!"

And we laugh. And the barman is coming in our direction, to our table, as if he is reading our minds or hearing our conversation from behind the bar, bearing on his tray a jug of martini. And we laugh, and he laughs and says, "You two on vacation?" and we say nothing, but continue laughing, and he pours the clear, powerful liquid into two new, large, chilled martini glasses, through a strainer, places very delicately two green, juicy olives on a stick with the emblem of the bar on them into each glass, wipes the rings from the oval, black, shiny table, and is leaving when John says, "You a Baptiss?"

"Nope." he says. I detect an accent.

"Catholic?" John asks.

"Do I look like one?"

"Church of England!" I say.

"I am a Protestant. Guess that makes me something like Church-of-Fengland, too! I'll buy that!"

"Would you by chance happen to know how many hymns there are in the hymnbook that the Anglicans use, or the Protestants? The book called *Hymns Ancient & Modern?*"

"Sure! Seven-hundred seventy-nine!"

"Goddamn!" John says, spluttering drink and spit on my clothes.

"Wanna hear all seven-hundred seventy-nine?"

"Goddamn!" John says.

"Oh no!" I say, fearing more singing.

"Hold on to this," John says.

"Thanks," the barman says, "but are you gentlemen leaving already?"

"Just thought I'd give you a little something for serving us, just thought . . ."

"Any time you gentlemen needs me again, just raise a finger, just raise a finger, just raise a finger . . ." And he folds the American twenty-dollar note and slips it into the top left pocket of his black waistcoat.

"God-*damn!*" John says.

"I'm going to look it up, the minute I get back to my house! The minute I get home," I say.

"Home! What a sweet word! We've made this goddamn bar our home, I'd say! And what a sweet home! Home-sweet-home, home-sweet-home."

"My mother had a square piece of cloth worked in crochet with the words *home sweet home* embroidered in it. Two birds that were red were at each side of the frame, and in the frame she had put a cross made out of a leaf from a coconut palm tree that the Vicar distributed to each member of the congregation one Palm Sunday. She kept this cross made outta palm-leaf in her Bible for fourteen years before she got married to my father; and she kept this crocheted motto, *home sweet home*, in the front-house over a mahogany cabinet. That mahogany cabinet she kept her silvers, cut-glass, and crystals in. And she never used them except on Easters and when somebody she liked got married. She served the food for the wake, to close members of her family, remaining uncles and aunts on both sides of her family tree, in these silvers and crystals the day my uncle came back up, swelled up and bloated from drowning. It was at the wake that I heard some fishermen-friends say my uncle should have learned how to float on the water, at least, if he couldn't swim. Float on the sea. Float on the water. Home sweet home! I think your Old Lady had a picture that said *home sweet home* too. But hers was a real picture in colour. A watercolour showing an English cottage with a thatched roof, like the leaves of the coconut palm tree. You remember that picture? Smoke was always coming out of the top of the roof, through a chimbley. And I always wondered if that wasn't the house of your Old Lady's dreams. And once when I went back home on vacation after twenty-five years, I visited her in the house you bought for her, and the house looked almost identical to the one in the home-sweet-home watercolour picture that was painted by an English-man, in blue and grey and brown. The picture is still hanging in the front-house of your Old Lady's new home. All those English pictures that we used to look at when we were growing up, showing us a world that we already knew from books, and which we saw, through those illustrations every day around us, those English pictures fitted-in to the landscape of our lives as if we had painted them ourselves. The painters born in Barbados, most of them, paint only blue skies and deep-blue sea water with a coconut tree leaning to one side sprouting up in the middle of the canvas. Barbadian art is nothing more than post cards for tourisses. I remember the girl, O-Mary. The girl who walked up to her knees in water going after her sheep and goats across the River Dee. And I understand why the man that wrote the poem and the man who painted the watercolour to illustrate the poem coloured the little girl's hair red. We have never seen women in Barbados with red hair, have we? To my mind, nobody ever dyed her hair red. Oh! Now I remember something! Do they play calypsos on the radio in Durham-North Carolina where you live? I just remember a calypso, one about what you were telling me, about the three men and the cow with horns. It's a calypso about a woman dancing too close to a man, and the man is not her boyfriend, nor the man she went to the dance with, and the calypsonian, who is a woman, is warning her not to allow this other man to horn her real man; and then the calypso uses other terms for horning. She says the Jamakians call it *burn*, or *bu'n*. It's a sweet calypso, but when I heard it the first time, I felt so sad, so sorry for men who find themselves in that predicament."

"You were, once."

"I forget. When I heard the calypso it was years after the apartment episode, so I didn't apply the meaning to myself. I feel sad, though, that a man could face that kind o' thing in real life, 'cause there are lots of stories from biblical times, and from even when we were growing up, of a man coming home and finding his woman, or his kip-miss, or even his wife, in bed with another man. And I always wondered what I would do, if that happened to me. What would you do? Have you ever found yourself in that situation? Would you kill the woman? Or the man?"

"Nothing."

"You won't kill the man? Or at least throw some lashes in his arse?"

"Nothing. It could happen to any man. As long as you're living, it could happen to you. Not a goddamn thing!"

"A woman who is your wife," I say. I say this with some cruel cynicism, because since I do not have a woman, and have not had a woman for years, I am feeling superior about the impossibility to be horned. "Or a woman you're living with and supporting, and you open your front door to your home and come home, as you are accustomed, and on this occasion you happen not to be making the amount o' noise you usually make when you come home, and you open the door to your bedroom, and *there*, right there, is a man in the saddle. In your bed. Lying-down on your woman or wife, grinding-away. And you would do nothing? That is not like you. That is not like a man. I could see that if the man in question was himself taking a little piece on-the-side with another woman, that his conscience and guilt might get the better of him; or if the man caught red-handed in your bed was a bigger man than you; or if the man was richer, and powerful, like a politician; or like is the case in Barbados with the wife working for a bank, and the bank manager starts getting a little piece; or usually as is the case, the wife is working in a haberdashery store, and the owner starts treating her good and getting a taste in return. Even the owner of a grocery store. You really would walk away and do nothing?"

"You didn't hear what I said? I said it could happen to any man."

"It happened to you? Where? In Italy?"

"I didn't say that. And I didn't say I would *walk away*. I said I wouldn't kill the woman, or the man. But what I would do is this. I would take off my jacket and my tie and my shoes, and my trousers, and lay-down beside the two o' them. Beside she and him. In the same bed. And pretend that nothing had-happen. And I would wait till the man put-back-on his clothes, trousers, shirt, socks, underwears, and tie; and I know that he *bound* to leave; and the moment he leave and go through the door, I would *paint her ass!*"

"So cruel? You're a cruel man."

"A cruel man? Not with blows. With *love*. And after I make love with her, I would put-back-on my clothes, get in my motor-car, and drive straight to my lawyer and begin proceedings. Then, I would turn-round in my motor-car and drive *straight* to that man's house, because Barbados is a small place, and I must know this man, where he live, perhaps me and him are friends;

147

and when I reach his house, be it a small chattel house or a big plantation house, or a mansion, I would enter, axe him for a drink, tell him me and him have to speak a few words in private, that we had-better go outside so his wife don't hear what I have to tell him, and when I got that son of a bitch in the backyard . . ." I feel he is talking about himself, and when he goes on, I am sure this is a real story; and I wonder why. John is contradicting himself? "I took out my gun and place one shot in his fucking head. 'Take that!' I told the son of a bitch, 'take that!' And I stood up over him, and finished my drink and I dropped the empty glass on the fucker laying-down there, in front o' me, dead. It's the Eye-talian experience in my blood. I like Eye-talians. A man do that to me? And get-off? It's the Eye-talian in me. They know about *amoray*."

"I didn't know. I thought you were joking. This happened to you when you were living in Italy?"

"Enough said," John snaps.

"Did this happen when you were living in France?"

"Every goddamn day! You open the paper *Il Figaro*, and you read that a man fucked with another man, and you see that man with his throat cut, and leff in the gutter. Or you see a man, usually well-dress, 'cause Eye-talians like their clothes and their *disegnatores*, silk tie and shirts with their initials worked-in on their cuffs or pocket, and very nice leather shoes. They're very well-dress, Eye-talians. You've heard about Eye-talian leather shoes, the finest in the world? Bruno Maglis?

148

Only thing, their shoes are not made for black people, and can't fit us too good, 'cause our feet is too broad. Broad feet and low instep. I don't really think that Hannibal did such a good job. I don't think he do his job properly when he crossed the fucking Alps! *In occulo altero Hannibal Alpam . . .*"

"*Transgresserat!*" I say. He smiles from ear to ear. "But doesn't that word, *transgresserat,* have a connection to *transgression,* in a figurative sense, although the strict sense is *crossing?* I suppose a crossing-over is a crossing-over, even if one is crossing the Alps, or crossing-over a man's woman!"

"But I begin telling you about the only other time, apart from my Old Lady's death, when I cried like a baby. At Gloria's funeral. I was telling you about Gloria. At the funeral, the church was *packed.* Gloria had friends. But I never imagined she had an army o' friends, nor so many. People like peas. All kinds. White. Black. Blue. Brown. Red. French-people, Wessindians living in Paris, and even some came over from London-England. First time I ever see a funeral at a church packed with people, and still people are stanning-up outside like if they are lining-up to go in a dance or a movie. People? She had two priests taking part. People in black. And people in mauve. All the men in black. Not like in the States where some son of a bitch going-appear at your funeral, a blessèd, sacred affair, dressed in a T-shirt and a pair o' bluejeans. And Adidas! None o' that slackness. Proper mourners in proper attire and

149

apparel. A proper funeral. A very lovely funeral. They sang in French, but everybody knows a burial-hymn when they hear one, regardless of the words sung in *français*! And they had me read a lesson, First Corinthians. And I went up in the part of the *église* by the altar and the sacristy, and climb the seven steps up to the lectern, and I tell you, those steps were more like seventeen or sixteen, and my two knees were wobbly, and I could hardly hold the page. It was the first time I realize how thin and fragile a page from the Bible is. First Corinthians. '*Now is Christ risen from the dead, and become the first-fruits of them that slept. For since by man came death, by man came also the resurrection of the dead.*' I read it in English. When I reach that part, the tears start to flow, and the page became blurred and I could see Gloria in her pink nightgown with her left bubbie drooping over the top of the nightgown-bodice, and how it was moving as she moved to take up another piece of the bacon that she had fried too hard, and I started to feel my tom-pigeon getting hard, and I started to feel dirty, nasty, and sinful. Here I am in a cathedral, in a French *église*, as she had the funeral service in a big cathedral in Paris. In this cathedral with droves o' people packing-down the church, like at a dance in Barbados, and my mind is back in that apartment watching Gloria in her pink nightgown. The rest of the words melted into one, like the water-rings we're leaving on this table, into one blurred line, like things look when you drop them in the sea, and the sea water makes them bigger than in real life. And the tears, Timmy, the tears, the tears. They had to rescue me from the lectern in the pulpit, or where I was, and lead me outside. Outside, it was cold; and an old lady who was-born in Barbados, but had-come-over to Paris to live, and to study piano lessons, administered smelling salts to me, to try to revive me. 'Here, son,' she says to me, talking with a real broad Barbadian accent after all the years she had spend in Paris, and with the vapour from her mouth almost hiding her from me and me from her. 'Take this. Is smelling salts. You love her *real-bad*, didn't yuh? Breathe-it-in. But don't breathe-it-in too deep. Yuh going-live-through this strategy, boy. Tek the smelling-salts.'"

"She died in the depths of winter? You were still married to the *parlez-vous* woman, and living in France?"

"It was just before I leff France. Just before I leff my first-wife Hyacinthe the *parlez-vous* woman and my three thrildren behind. One afternoon, me and the wife taking a walk through the Shan-deleezays, and who am I going to butt-up-on but this same old Barbadian woman. She see me and she lowers her head. I stop right in front of her. And she raises her two eyes and shake her head, and look me straight in my two eyes, and say, 'Them smelling salts *revive* you real fast, eh, smart-boy? The girl not dead quite going on a week, and you tek-up with this one, a'ready? The smelling salts work real fast, eh?' And she move off. I felt like a piece o' shit.

151

Hyacinthe, who is a real *parlez-vous* woman and don't understand a word of English, is smiling and nodding her head at this old Barbadian woman, as she is cursing my ass, Hyacinthe not knowing what had-pass between me and that old Barbadian lady. And to this day, I don't have the nerve to tell her. Gloria was a woman-and-a-half. A beautiful woman. Sometimes, now that she dead, I wonder if I shouldn't have-followed my mind in regards to my real feelings at the beginning, and axe her for a piece . . . No disrespect to the dead, though."

"God rest her soul. No disrespect . . ."

"May she rest in peace! Goddamn!"

"You loved her."

"I loved her."

"Cousin, or no cousin?"

"Cousin, or no cousin. I should, under-the-circumstances, have-at-least axed her how she woulda feel about my axe-ing her the question. But she is dead. And it is too late. And it goes with her in the grave, in the ground hard as iron, so hard that when the coffin hit the bottom of the grave, I thought it was going to break-up in pieces. It was a strange thought to think. The morning was so cold, so cold, that I had to keep my two hands inside my pockets, and when I breathe, only vapour coming outta my mouth."

"I don't ever want to die in this cold country. At least, not during the winter," I say, and make a dramatic shiver.

"You have no choice. At your age, what you think

your chances is that you won't drop-dead on Yonge Street, one o' these mornings whilst you are walking? One in one-hundreds? Or one-in-ten, to be generous?"

"In all my time here, I never attended more than *one* funeral."

"Nobody that you know ever died? You don't know anybody who died? In all these years you been living here? It's because you're 'sociating with only young people. 'Cause people drop dead every day!"

"A few acquaintances much younger than me *have* passed-away. But I don't like to think about death. A few acquaintances. But nobody close. One or two women. But no relation. In this country, from the time I came here, I had nobody close. You realize that when I first came here, with all the West Indians living here as students, and nurses and domestics making up most of the immigrants, *not one of them* was a grandmother? Or a grandfather?"

"Your life here is not natural. My life down there in Durm-North Carolina is a little natural. To-besides it warm in Durm. But with you, you might be looking for a second-spring. Are you looking for a second-spring? You like younger women. You may not admit it. A man your age, and my age, usually likes younger women to make them feel younger. The ego." He smiles as he says this, teasing me and not teasing; but he has made a wound, nevertheless, and it causes me to think. He has made a wound, deep and raw and bleeding. He smiles, and I see gold showing discreetly at the right side of his mouth. And I smile, remembering the ways of Barbadian emigrants to countries in the southern hemisphere, Aruba, Curaçao, Venezuela, and Panama. All his original teeth are still in his mouth. The gold is only a filling. Some European sophistication he has picked up in his travels. Those men from our village, emigrants who went *south*, to Curaçao and to Aruba to help find and refine oil, returned home after their two-year contract ended, and entered Barbados with their pockets loaded with guilders, and their mouths gilded in gold, speaking a version of American twang none of us could understand. But we small boys imitated it, in awe at their ease with a new language, American or Dutch, both equally broken like the teeth they had replaced with gold, just as they had lived their former lives speaking broken English when they wished to be impressive making an argument. John's mouth flashes me back to that of my uncle's, on my father's side, who had come back from Caracas and Panama where he went to attend cattle and later attend the men who dug trenches, and who talked about the size of steaks he ate, big as a house and red as blood, and to help build the Panama Canal; and he came back with new suits made in Holland of the finest fabric, hundreds of guilders in cash in his pockets, pink silk shirts the colour of women's dresses and nightgowns, a colour which men, which our time said was reserved only for women. And this new liberated man started calling us *hombres* and *compañeros*, and saying *qué pasa, qué pasa?* when an old lady in the village told him, "Good morning." And calling the rest of us who did not know those Spanish words, and who had not travelled, *niggers* and *nigeros*, remembering words he had learned in barrios where dogs lived with men and women. And we prayed that the oil-refining scheme and its companies would take him back quick to the rough barracks of Caracas and Panama, which he said housed only tough *hombres* and *compañeros*.

John is still speaking about old men in love with younger women, but my mind wanders back to those times when the men in our village tried their luck with gold and oil and new young words.

"A young woman *don't* make an older man younger," he is saying. "Quite *au contraire!*"

"An old man gets younger with a young woman," I argue.

"The old man has to work too hard! All that working usually brings on a heart-affection. Heart-attack, if it doesn't kill him, or make him more older!"

"*Au contraire!*" I say, imitating him.

My mind wanders very often these days. But it wandered often when I was in elementary school, and at Combermere School for Boys, and later at Harrison College; and it wandered every day of the four years I spent at Trinity College here in Toronto. It has been wandering ever since, and with its wandering I fall off into a small sleep, a doze. At regular intervals during this lingering afternoon with John, I have been dozing off and on, but not allowing John to feel that his tales of existence and experience in Brooklyn and Durham, North Carolina, are not gripping my attention. Dozing off is my habit. While reading. While drinking. While eating. And once, when I was a much younger man, a woman accused me to my face of dozing off while making love when she was on the brink of an orgasm. I left her with no satisfaction. I do not remember her name. If decorum and propriety had not buckled me down and kept my tongue in silence, I would have told her that it was merely my peaceful appreciation of *her* love, and my passive disposition under the writhing, demanding up-and-downs, the pistons of my creaking mechanism, that caused me to express my savouring her passion in that desultory manner – by dozing – and that I had a need to recover from the exhaustion by taking a quick nap, taking that nose-dive of a doze. I make fun in these words of that accusation laid at my doorstep, years ago; but this is merely an attempt at erasure. The accusation has corroded the virility I hinted at earlier in my narrative to John, and I live from day to day with its bruising condemnation.

John is talking while I am wandering in the thoughts of my personal history, while his voice comes at me, like the soft sprinkle of cold water from melting ice, falling into my neck, rousing me to the uncomfortableness of staying awake long enough to catch the thread of his story. ". . . Paris was cold and I spoke no French and she won't learn Barbadian or English," I hear him saying; and I shake my head to drive the sleep from it, and to try to put his words in some focus and context. "We went home to Barbados twice on holiday, though. She spend her time at the *Alliance Française*, and I spend my time in the rum-shop around the corner from the beach where me and you used to sit and look at the sea. She never tried to learn to speak my language . . ."

The bar becomes like the night back home in the island, in the thick darkness, sitting in the front-house with the flickering wick of the kerosene lamp which seems to get brighter with the sweet, lulling voice of Ella Fitzgerald; and the light from the fake Tiffany lamps fades and we are swallowed in almost total, crêpe-like darkness, with only our eyes flashing. The entire bar is dark now, and soft, and cradled with the voice coming through the speaker of the Rediffusion box. And, in the darkness, a voice drones and I am carried away on another wave with its memory. "Ten thrildren!" he is saying now. "Ten thrildren from three different wives and a spouse, as they call it nowadays. Imagine, imagine one man having ten thrildren from three different wives and the woman he is living with now. From the *parlez-vous* woman, two of the loveliest thrildren you can imagine. Forty and thirty-nine is their ages, which makes me a goddamn old man, if yuh look at it that way. Monique and Faye, forty and thirty-nine, two of the prettiest thrildren you can imagine, two thrildren that I raised by myself when they were thrildren, even attended the classes in having babies and in breathing properly during childbirth, and in giving birth to babies, conducted in French, *s'il vous plaît!* Here I am, in this clinic, this *clinique* in Paris, surrounded by bare women, all women surrounding me, and the instructor is talking in French, and I am sitting-down rubbing my wife's belly. And you know something? Every time I lay my two hands on the woman's belly, I am getting an erection! I didn't give a damn about those horny French-men attending the classes, but it was the women I was embarrassed over, in case they saw the stiffness in my pants. And I did this for about three months, waiting for the child to born, and two times a week I am sitting-down on the cold floor in this *clinique* listening to all this French and not understanding one fucking word except the French for *belly*,'cause my mind was on sex. We had sex right up to the day the child was borned. They say it is good for the mother, but what is good for the mother is more better for the gander. After that, it was Italy and the Eye-talians. Spent a little time in Rome-Italy, and had three just-as-pretty *bambinos*, Roberto, Ricardo, and Umberto, thirty-three, thirty-two, and thirty-one; and me behaving as if I am a fucking child-making machine! A sociologist, a psychiatrist, and a' anthropologist, those three are. I don't know where they get their brains from. Perhaps from me. Perhaps more from their Eye-talian mother. In that order, a sociologist, a psychiatrist, and a' anthropologist, all-three professors at the same place, the University of Rome, the university that Mussolini build. So, I been making geniuses. That is my contribution to mankind. Then, I get fed-up with Rome and Italy and Eye-talians, including the women. In the ten years that I live in Rome-Italy, drinking Scotch and eating spaghetti, I picked up very little Eye-talian, and my wife was fluent in English and French. I could never understand why in all those countries, I had to learn their goddamn language, as if their language was *something*, something special, and my language was shit. All the time, none of my thrildren made a' effort to learn Barbadian or to know anything Barbadian, Barbadian customs and culture, or Barbadian food. Ain't that a bitch? It was as if I was living only half my life, operating on one engine or cylinder, trying to talk to everybody in a foreign language, and not one fucker wanting to learn *my* language! So I split. Not that the language-thing was the only cause for me splitting, but it must have been connected. Then, it was the South, after Brooklyn. The South. The deep South. The South is the best place for an *hombre* like me to live in; and I get a job in a firm, in a corporation of social workers and therapisses . . ."

I begin to pay attention; and I think I remember that he had said earlier that he was in another profession, but I am not sure. "On the train up north, to get to Sick Thrildren's Hospital, up here from New York, where I left my car, after driving up from Durm-North Carolina, all I could see was snow and more snow, like if I was really in a plane flying through clouds. Snow and snow, and the occasional lake or river, frozen-up anyhow, and almost the same colour as the snow . . . we pulled out from, from Penn Station and then hit Yonkers . . . and after Hudson we came into Albany-Rensselaer, where a lot o' people got off, and it made me think of trains and carriages in Germany during the war, and trains taking people to concentration camps . . . probably because of what was on my mind, regarding the hospital, and for being here . . ." I do not know why he is here. I plan to ask him, and then I forget. His words wash away my deep curiosity to know, in this flood of words. I have to know why he is here. ". . . It was Schenectady that put me right back home, that remind me of back home, 'cause I could swear that I remember how every Sunday morning we used to listen to a preacher preaching outta Schenectady on the radio. Don't you remember Schenectady? Was it Quito or Schenectady? Schenectady that was mention in the radio church services broadcast from the States?" I am listening to him now, and listening to the smooth voice coming through the speaker of the short-wave wireless, when we had moved up in the world from the rented Rediffusion box, and were now huddled around a "private set" as we called the short-wave wireless, made in Holland. The private set was attached to a very long piece of wire almost as long as the clothesline in the backyard, but this line of wire, the aerial, was strung inside the front room of the house, bringing the full blast of power in the word of God, his anger with black people who tuned in Sunday after Sunday, sinners in fear of hell, in longer sermons that shook the heart more deeply than the ones preached by the Vicar of the Anglican church. "Schenectady, New York!"

"Greater power in words," I say.

"Greater sins to report."

"Sweeter voices, always sweeter voices! Southern voices preaching the gospel to black people!"

"My God! Imagine! Is only now that I realize and can see that we was listening to Southern voices telling us about hell and brimstone and repentance! Is only now that I understand our attraction to those voices, that I realize what is the association with those Southern voices of the nineteen-thirties and nineteen-forties."

"There were white voices, looking back now."

"There were sweeter voices preaching beyond the seas, than the voice of the Vicar."

"White cracker voices . . ."

". . . that brought the gospel to Barbados and the Caribbean!"

"Sweet preaching Sunday voices, coming like a long river of molasses capsized over the private set, pouring out Sunday after Sunday."

"Schenectady, New York!" I say.

"And after Schenectady was Amsterdam, goddamn! That's a place I never visited while I was in Europe, and I wonder why. Utica, Rome, Syracuse, making me feel I

161

was travelling through Italy again; or going back in ancient times, before I was there. But I *beginned* telling you about my wives," he says. "And the South being the best place for a' *hombre* like me to live, where a man can make real money, and still remain lonely as hell in the South. That is the South for you. I work for a corporation of social workers, sort o' activisses-like who call themselves therapisses, therapists; and I been working with this firm *for years* without a licence. A bunch o' therapists, sociologists, and psychiatrists. I even tried my hand at some psychiatriss-work, and seeing as how the firm is so well-known and so well-regarded, my licence problem was absolved by the name of the institution I work for, and I did not have to prove that I was licensed, and did not have a licence. Nobody gives a goddamn if you have a licence, or if you don't have a goddamn licence, or so I feel. Nobody cares. But my work was supervised by one of the real psychiatriss who have a licence. And I wasn't engaged in telling anybody, in particular a woman, that she needed a special kind o' medication, and I didn't put anybody on pills. Just talk. Psychiatriss-talk. Apart from liking the work I do in Durm-North Carolina, there is things about the place that I like, like pecans and Virginia hams and *real* Southern-fried chicken, none o' this Kentucky Fried shit! And the smell of the place! The *smell* of the place, the smell of patchouli all over the place, on the clothes of the women, on their underwears, on their bodies, what a smell, patchouli! And the sight of the magnolia trees, those goddamn magnolia trees! Sometimes, they make me rage with anger, like the type o' black rage that you read about in *Ebony* magazine. Magnolia trees! And you know, one night I was relaxing with my woman, and we had-just-take a bath together, with patchouli bubbles in the water, and was drinking some white wine, and she put on this record . . . that was when I was still in love with magnolia trees. Well, she put on this record, and I hear the words, and something come into my body, my whole body, in my heart, I could feel it like a spasm, hearing Billie Holiday for the first time, singing about the magnolia trees. And after hearing Billie Holiday sing about the magnolia trees, my tom-pigeon *refuse* to get hard. Brother, I could not get hard. And I was goddamn scared I never would get a hard-on again. We listened to Aretha Franklin after Billie Holiday. And I start to feel a little more better, and more peckish. And my tom-pigeon start to rise again. But those goddamn beautiful magnolia trees that overhang the street and make it look like *duss* before it is even six o'clock in the evening. The magnolia trees, you never see them, 'cause after listening to a song like the one Billie Holiday sing, you can't really look up at them and see them as a normal tree, for with the words in the song, you cannot ever see their beauty again. Except you're white. Black bodies hanging from a branch of a tree . . ."

"What made you say that?" I ask.

"It's from the song," John says.

"Billie Holiday is a black singer?" I ask.

"And my woman didn't goddamn tell me!"

"Billie, Billie Holiday . . . Lady Day."

"And the food. The amount o' food that Southerners can eat, the men *and* the women, especially the women. In my books they are the best goddamn women in the *whirl*! I like my women big, and heavy and solid and sturdy. So gimme a sturdy woman any day – or night, for that matter – in preference to some thin-ass, twiggy-type o' broad walking-'bout on gangways as fashion-models swinging their ass from side to side and not doing nothing for me, Jack! This woman does nothing for me. A big woman is like a tonic, like a man's blessing, especially when she puts her weight fair-and-square on you. Goddamn!" And he raises his voice, and slaps his thick palms. And people in the bar look at us. "Goddamn! All that weight! That lovely weight! And I am a small man by comparison, as you can see. Young age in a woman? Young women? You can keep that! But gimme the weight, any day, baby! Avoirdupois. It must be the pork chops and fry-chicken. Don't you like big women, like those big Amurcan mommas? They remind me of Barbados; though, as I say, I don't go back to Barbados too often, nor to the Wessindies, barring the two times I take the *parlez-vous* lady there, when she spend all her time at the *Alliance Française* polishing-up her French instead o' talking in my language, or coming with me in the rum-shop and learn

164

how to drink a rum. And it really burned my ass 'cause it was after we had-arrive too late, after my Old Lady died, when I got the message concerning her death too late to get there and lift her head. But I tell you something this evening right here in Toronto. The very next goddamn time I go back there, or you hear that I gone back there, to Barbados or the Wessindies, it is in a goddamn mahogany box with silver strappings and a silver breastplate on that box bearing my name and date-o'-birth. Rest-in-fucking-peace! *Adios! Adieu!* But getting back to the women of the South; the women of the South, they remind me of a calypso by Lord Kitchener, "Sugar-Bum-Bum." Too-sweet! All the way up North on that Amtrak train, after I turn-off the overhead light that I was reading the latest copy of *Ebony* magazine with, and I close my two eyes, and right through my mind pass this woman, this big, lovely Southern momma, when she walks in the house, the floorboards rumble and does-creak; and when she lays-down on me, goddamn! The sweetness of her weight! The sweetness I see in that woman! How-come you don't say much about women? You're talking to *me*, ya know?"

I find it easy to picture him deep in the South, in Durham, North Carolina, or in Atlanta, Georgia, or in Austin, Texas; and I am able to do this because in all this time we have been drinking, and he is talking about France and Italy and Germany, the pictures of his narrative are drawn with a heavier touch of the language from the South than from those countries in Europe. And I think that, perhaps, he never lived in them. For the language he has retained from those countries is not a real language, not a true language, but merely his retention of words, tastes. And when he is talking about back home in the island, he speaks in an honest, native, broad and flat Barbadian accent, much like the old Barbadian lady who gave him the smelling salts in Paris at Gloria's funeral. But out of all these voices that he hides his emotions in, tracing the French, the Italian, and the German, like a spider's web, there is no more powerful web of enchantment that captures that afternoon on the beach at Paynes Bay. His own language makes clear those chapters in the past that he is laying before me, on this shiny, round, black table. I am beginning to wonder how much of his talk he expects me to believe, how much he expects me to trust, out of all his stories which have me laughing and sad. But I know he expects me to trust all of them. We both know that time erodes truth and memory; doubting and accepting. But I am also intrigued by his life; and once I laughed so loudly at what he was telling me that I forgot we are still sitting in this bar, now crowded, and that we are not alone on that deserted beach. Some women fresh from work look, on these occasions, in our direction, stare, do something with their eyes and the shape of words on their red lips, and I think I hear the word "*Americans!*" from their lips, the word standing for something else unmentionable, and spoken with a flat venom of distaste about the noise we two old black men are making in the quiet, dimly lit bar with the fake Tiffany lamps. I can feel their distaste because I am more acquainted with it, their disapproval of our loudness. We are the only ones who speak and laugh that others can hear. Around us is the whispering of church and concert congregation. At times like this, after all these years, it is the quietness of this city that makes me feel different, that makes me shiver with that difference – and still I must walk these lonely streets, as I watch all these people passing me, without one word, without one smile. And all I see as I watch them is a grimace, if I watch too closely or try to smile a greeting. But I might be imagining . . . this quiet unspokenness bordering upon boredom and psychotic silence, and the cleanliness of the city.

The barman walks smiling from behind the safety of the bar, which he polishes with a cloth that is turning less white from the cleaning with each span of dabbing and wiping up of water on the counter and the wiping up of spilt drinks, and is now standing beside John and me. He is changing the ashtray yet another time, although it has not been used, in a gesture of service and dedication. He has the small round tray in his left hand, flat to his chest, and his right hand is deep into his right trousers pocket, jingling the change of his tips.

"Now, this is what I want you to do for me this time," John is telling the barman, who listens as he runs the cloth across the silk of the water on our table. John's speech takes on a friendly slur. He is now drunk. The barman mistakes this for merriment. It is the season. "Now," John says, and stops, as if this is the end of what he intends to say. Words are coming with greater difficulty, slothful and slow. "Now. If you don't mind me saying so. If you don't mind me saying so. And I don't. Wish. And I don't wish. To tell you how to do your job. To tell you how to do your job. 'Cause I been a waiter, a barman, myself. In some of the best bars in the Big Apple. You *know* the Big Apple! And I'll be god-damned. Be goddamn mad. If some son of a bitch from off the street comes into my bar. And tells me how to do my job. If you see what I'm saying." The words are coming easier now. "But this time, this time, I want to axe you to do me a little favour. A little favour is all I axe, if you see what I'm saying. This time, when you make the next two double martinis, pass the vermouth bottle, *unopen*, over the glass, and measure-off two drops, two drops of Chivas in each martini glass, and then pour-off the ice *and* the Chivas; and fill-er-up, Joe! Fill-er-up! Fill-er-up! I'm here talking to my ace-boon, this son of a bitch who I haven't rested my two goddamn eyes on in forty, no, *fifty* years! Half a-goddamn-century! Not since me and him were small. Me and him born in Barbados, went-school at the same schools, done the same things, got-into the same goddamn trouble, was unseparated like two twins; he was flogged by my mother, him and I; and I got my backside tarred by *his* mother, me and him, if you see where I'm coming from. So, this son of a bitch comes here, to reside; and I find myself travelling the *whirl*! We just met. Right here. On the street out there. Me and him. On Yonge Street. A minute ago. I'm ploughing through your goddamn snow, like a snow-removal, and into this goddamn son of a bitch, my ace-boon, I bounced. He. Him. Look at him! Rambling in the white-people thoroughfare, and nearly knocked me flat on my ass in all that snow outside. So, where you from, y'all? Where you from?"

"Sydney."

"You're from Australia?"

"Nova Scotia. Sydney, Nova Scotia."

"Knew you had some Wessindian in you!"

"Grandmother."

"Would you take one with us?"

"Don't-mind-if-ah-do!"

"Pour yourself a goddamn drink, fella. Goddamn! Ain't this something? We be taking-over North Amurca, if y'all not careful in this country." And he glances at the three women nearby, chatting and giggling, as Buddy the barman agrees to follow the instructions for making the martinis; and as Buddy leaves, John glances at the three women again. "Look at those three fine foxes, will ya? Check-em-out, brother, 'cause there sure ain't no harm in looking! I'm a legs-man, myself. What you is?"

"Breasts. Bubbies."

"Goddamn! First indication you give me that you like women! Gimme the legs any time. Legs and avoir-dupois."

"I like the fingers, too. Fingers do some funny things to me, especially fingers with long fingernails that don't have nail polish . . ."

"Come closer. Hold over, 'cause I don't want those three chicks to hear. Check it out. The one. In the. Black stockings. Pantyhose. With the red shoes. It's a good thing. They can't. Read our minds. Isn't she something? Isn't she just something? I am a legs-man, any time."

"There was a time when a woman's fingers would do some funny things to me. Now, I concentrate on the breasts. Saying this for a woman to know, we could be charged with some kind of sexual assault. In this country, a man could be accused . . ."

"Goddamn! But I'll be goddamned if any mother-fucker gonna tell *me* I can't admire a woman's legs!"

"But still. The things we're saying in private and in secret, if they were known by any of those three women . . ."

"I love to see a woman with *well-form* teeth. Strange, how men have these little likes and dislikes that they can't express in the open. You know how *obsess* I am with legs and feet and teeth, and *weight* . . . And Jesus Christ, all that avoirdupois! Now, I am not a jeans-person, attracted to tight-fitting latex pants that cycliss wear. For a woman to turn up at my place, dressed in tight shiny spandex pants, my mind turns off, and my desire disappears. Dissipates. If you see where I am coming from."

"I wonder if women talk about men the way we are observing these three chicks, two old men, sitting down in this bar, undressing these three women. Come close. Listen. *Once.* A woman. She was. About thirty-nine. Or forty . . ."

"Look-look-look! Don't look too obvious. But the one on your left. In the white, shiny hose, the colour of silver. See her? My God! The *parlez-vous* woman, my Hyacinthe, was just like her! If she wasn't in France, I woulda *swear* it is my first-wife sitting at that table! Goddamn!"

". . . about forty. She would cook dinner, and we would sit down at the table with white linen tablecloth, or a cloth like damask, with white watermarks in the pattern. What do you call that kind of tablecloth? Lace? Anyhow, she always had candles, white candles like those big, fat white ones we used to light in the chancel of the Cathedral Church, you remember? And she always served white wine. She knew a lot about wines. Dinner usually was steak fried, with all the blood run—ning out of it, with onions and broccoli and always with mashed potatoes. She liked mashed potatoes. While I am eating, I am feeling peckish, and not only for her food. After we eat the steak with the blood running out of it, she would serve dessert topped with brandy. I am drinking my brandy, and I am still feeling *peckish*. I have never told this to anybody before. Anyhow. After we eat, she would go into the bathroom, and come back out in a kind o' shortie-pyjamas made out of white silk, and

171

then we would have some more white wine, and then she would say to me, just plain so, with no foreplay or play or touching, "Do you want to do it?" And sudden-so, the urge would leave me. Rubbing me, kissing me, massaging me, sticking me with her fingernails, *nothing*, not a damn thing would make me have the urge as I first had the urge of peckishness. This went on happening for more than six months. 'Don't worry,' she would tell me, 'it happens.' It happens perhaps; but it never happened to me before, and the more . . ."

"Didn't you see a doctor?"

"A doctor? I wasn't sick!"

"Didn't you see your family doctor?"

"I don't have a family. All the years in Toronto, I never had a doctor. Even if I had-had a doctor, I couldn't as a man go to a doctor and tell him that I can't have an erection! Are you out of your fucking mind? What would he think of me, a big black man like me?"

"Another trick she coulda used woulda been to wrap the steak round your tom-pigeon."

"On my tom-pigeon? The steak with the blood running out?"

"On your penis. Steak, but preferably cold, is the best cure for sterility, by putting it on your tom-pigeon."

"I just couldn't go to a doctor. Not to a white doctor. Imagine what that doctor would say about a man like me!"

"A black doctor, then. They have any black doctors in Canada?"

172

"A black doctor? That's worse, man! A *black* doctor? Can you imagine a man like me, in Toronto's small black community, going to a black doctor, and telling that black doctor that I can't get it up? A *black* doctor? I would be the laughing-stock of the whole black community! This doctor may talk. Everybody in his club and his church would hear about my ailment and affliction. No patient-doctor privilege would save my arse, man!" John is laughing. "It really bothered me, not knowing what to do, to cure this thing. For more than six months, she went on holding me like if I was a baby, saying, 'Don't worry, it happens'; and all the time making me kiss her breasts with her brassieres on, through the lace, and she rubbing the various parts of my body with oils from the Body Shop. My tom-pigeon still won't stannup, for nothing. I started reading books. *The Joy of Sex, The Joy of an Orgasm, The New Joy of Sex, Sex and the Male Organ,* and *Orgasms Galore!* She lent me *Sex as You Want It* and still I couldn't do nothing. But the worst part was that I feel-sure she told her girl friends about me. A black man who can't handle the situation. I know she did. Her girl friends started looking at me, and giggling. You know the way a woman can look at a man and start giggling? Has this ever happened to you? And I am only asking you because you and me grew up together. I could never ever ask a Canadian about this. This ever happened to you?"

"Goddamn!"

"Breasts have, however, remained my weakness. I only have to see a woman's brassieres, not even the bare breasts, especially when she is under the shower. And when you talk about a woman in the sea or in a swimming pool, and the water soaks her bathing-suit, and the nipples start to show-through the bra, or a woman athlete running a race, Jesus Christ! The moment I see the nipples . . ."

"Goddamn! You need help, brother, if you see what I'm saying. You seriously need help. Not that I am criticizing you. I am merely saying you's a man in need of help, sexuality-wise!"

"I suffered through those long six months with that woman, never mentioning it to anybody, and wouldn't, in case people start laughing at me. People usually laugh at these things when you can't perform. I know men who tell me that they could go with a woman for five hours. *Five hours. Five hours?* Jesus Christ, man, not even a horse could do that! That is almost a whole working-day! But even though I feel that a normal man can't *do-it* for five hours, still I can't say anything against that man. While I was seeing that woman's breasts while eating the steak, everything was fine. But the moment she goes into the bathroom, and comes back-out wearing a shortie-nightgown, my tom-pigeon falls. Flat."

"I don't mean to emasculate you further, or come on strong in the way of criticizing you," John says. His voice and his manner have changed. It is like waves rushing in and onto the beach in a wild surge, and then falling back into the sea, slowly and in a clear, sober run to the sea. He is looking straight at me, with clear, focused eyes. "I am acquainted with the myth that men like me and you have to live under. We's *suppose* to be kingpins in bed. And if you see what I'm saying, then you will understann that it is even written-about in books, about men like me and you. But you should have-seen a goddamn doctor. Having said that, I know that men like me and you don't go to doctors to seek *that* kind o' help and assistance. It *don't* look good. We is he-men, regardless o' age. And we have to behave like he-men. The things we're saying is things that nobody should ever hear-about; things that we have to hide from certain people; things that would, if they are known, make us look small, like small men. Is the same thing about going in a men's washroom with a lotta white boys peeing, and hiding their instruments and tom-pigeons, and looking at you outta the sides of their eyes while they are peeing, and measuring you with their glances, to see if the myth and the fear of the myth is justified, and . . ."

"That's why when I go in a men's room, I always use a cubicle, with a door that closes, and locks, as if I am using the toilet, and not going just to pee."

"Goddamn!"

"Just in case a white boy sees my tom-pigeon, and it doesn't measure-up in the eyes of *his* myths. It is a hard thing. Is a hard thing that men like me and you have to bear all this myth and fear, as you say. But getting back to the woman who used to invite me to candlelight dinners of rare steak. It made me *very ashamed* to know I couldn't *perform* under those romantic circumstances. And this woman was the most sexy-looking woman I ever known! Do you think that women talk about these things, measuring men, comparing men, sex-wise, and size-wise, as you would say? Women *couldn't* talk about these things! Jesus Christ, have a heart!"

"Women, far's my knowledge goes, not only talk about these things, comparison-wise, but they give other women your measurements. And your performance-quotients. And your complete statistics. And your frequencies, as if they are putting those other women on guard against you. Believe me, brother. There is nothing that a woman don't talk about about a man, to other women. Don't look now! Look when it is safe. Look-look-look. The one with the black stockings. You see those legs? Let me tell you something about legs, and about love and making love to a woman who have lovely legs. First you take a deep breath to control yourself. And when you get on top of a woman with nice legs, try to think of *anything*, but what you happen to be doing. Anything in the whirl, but take your full mind offa making love. You got to learn how to control yourself, brother. You gotta control yourself. *Control* is the word. You see them legs? If you do not control yourself, your body and your mind and your thoughts, you will make the mistake of coming before the woman is ready to come, if you see where I'm coming from.

You mentioned the Chinese woman. But you mentioned her once, and you never mentioned her again. Did you ever . . . you know what I mean . . . with the Chinese?" I refuse to answer him. I hope he has forgotten the story I told him hours ago. He ignores me, and says, "Chinese women are masters of the art of control. Control. The more you are able to take your mind off the present predicament, the more control you have, and the more longer you are going to last, through thought-association. But not association with the project at hand. Because women prefers the passion and emotion of the whole thing, whilst a man have a tendency to jump-on, *bang-bang!*, have a cigarette, put on his clothes, done-with-that, and leave. On the other hand, a woman need tenderness and something-else that cause that lingering experience to last, if you see what I'm saying. Men have been *horned* for this negligence."

"I can't talk about these things, certainly not to any tom-dick-and-harry; and if you weren't here, I probably wouldn't be able to say it; and it would have *stuck* in my conscience and consciousness for years without being talked about. And even talking about it now, I feel that somebody, a woman, any of these three women nearby, is hearing what I am saying. That would bring back the embarrassment I was embarrassed with, when it first happened."

"Legs! Gimme legs any day!"

"Breasts is my speed."

"But didn't you just said you can't bear to see breasts, even in a swimming pool?"

"I like teeth, too."

"Are you a dentist? To like teeth? Or a' orthodonnist? For me, is pure legs. Legs, legs, and more legs. And the weight. That avoirdupois."

"Now that I think about it, I think it was the colour," I say. John becomes alert. "The colour, in a cultural sense, an ethnic sense. I am talking about the aesthetics of colour."

"What the fuck you talking about, brother?" John says. "Colour have nothing to do with it. You don't have anything 'gainst *white* women, do you?"

"I mean the colour of the shortie-nightie she wears after she goes into the bathroom, and comes back out and asks me, 'Do you want to do it?' I mean that. In my mind I want to hold her soft and touch her soft and say things to her that are soft, that I read in books. And even say some of the things I read in the sex-books she gave me to read. But I always feel funny, scared; as if somebody is listening to me, like the same man who wrote the sex-book. Embarrassed. Less than a man. It isn't nothing against her colour as a person, is only against the colour she choose to wear, and then her sympathy which is a thing that a man like me can't handle. 'Don't worry, darling, it happens.' When she calls me 'darling,' that is when I change. I start feeling real cruel, and want to hit her, or 'buse her, or tell her hard things to make her stop calling me 'darling,' and using other endearing terms. With my tom-pigeon not rising, I feel she is really laughing at me."

"Is this the same woman who accused you of dozing-off whilst making love? The Chineewoman? Or is this a different woman? If you see what I'm saying, I am saying that the three women you are talking to me about might be *one and the same woman*. You see what I mean? But I am not here to analyze you, nor put you under therapy. I am here to visit a hospital, Sick Kids; and you and me are here to get drunk, blind-drunk on this reunion." This is my chance to ask him more about his sudden appearance in Toronto. This is my chance to clear up his long stories of the life he has spent in Europe. This is my chance. But, after all, it was he who could swim. And I am the little boy who stood and watched him walk on his hands, like a crab.

So, all I say is "That is what I mean. Meeting you in this reunion is important. Because in forty-something years, as I told you already, I couldn't find one person, certainly not a Canadian, man nor woman, regardless, that I could talk these things with, and not feel embarrassed. So, I agree that this is a reunion, a happy meeting. But it means more to me than that. It means being able to see the vacuum in my life, the lack o' meaning in my life, the half-life I been living all the time while thinking that I was a successful person. I wonder if we are the only men in this bar with these problems? Are we the only men with these problems, just-because we are black men, of a certain age?"

"Well, I really don't know. You may think that in my practice, un-licence as it is, that I would be in a position to answer all *your* questions. Most of the clients and people that I see are white people. White people have different problems to black people. As least, they come to me with different problems. Black men don't come to a black therapist to discuss something which we all take for granted. So, it is the women who tell me about their husbands and men, tell me different things. And the woman who tell you about falling-off in a light sleep whilst you should-been *performing like a man*, she was only telling you the truth. Just the truth. It hurts. It hurts like hell, like shite. But you have to live with it, as you lived with it all these years, before you see me this afternoon. No *consolation*, but the truth, if you see what I am saying."

"If I could ask you one final question. A personal question, a very personal question. Could I ask you if you went-through anything like what I was telling you?"

"Goddamn! You're getting into my private business now! You want a' answer from a professional? Or from a man?"

"*Your* experiences."

"Well, lemme tell you something, kid. And lemme tell it to you in the form of a few questions. But before I do, lemme order another martini, and this gonna-be my last. What about you? I gotta get back to Sick Kids. I think this is my last, as I have some things to do when I get back to that hospital, and before I go back to the hotel."

Now, once more, is my chance. But I do not take it, and ask him why. Why is he here? Time, in this bar, which has brought us close, after all these years, has also washed us in two different directions. I no longer see him as my best friend. Time has washed away that closeness. I feel he is my therapist. But I know that I still have to ask why he is here.

Buddy catches sight of our waving hands, nods his head, smiles, takes the cigarette from his lips, and comes over. John is lighting a cigar. As Buddy passes beside the table with the three women, one of them says something to him. It is the one wearing the silver pantyhose. He takes our order, and just before he moves away, John offers a round of drinks to the table with the three beautiful women. They are quieter now, talking in low voices; and sometimes their faces take on a serious manner, as if they are discussing children or jobs; and they do not laugh as often as we do, or as often as they were doing earlier when the evening was hilarious and the light from the fake Tiffany lamps spread its soft fingers through their hair and on the rich, deeply coloured material in their dresses and their woollen sweaters which hold the colours of late autumn in a richness close to Christmas.

"Which one you think sent us the drinks?" the woman in the silver hose asks her friends. I hear her whisper.

"The one with the cigar."

"I think it's the other one," the third one says.

"We'll order them a round, too."

"Not yet. Too soon. Would make it look as if we are . . ."

"Well, we'll do it just as we are ready to leave."

"That's better!"

I do not know if they have exchanged more remarks then these, for I have only heard the beginning, and we do not pay any more attention to them. They have reknitted their own circle of conversation and talk, and are like three islands close in a sea of blue warm water, lapping at the shore and leaving smiling waves as their teeth show, as their laughter ebbs like the retreating waves amongst them.

"Lemme tell you something," John says, striking the third match to light his cigar, "as I was about to. And tell it to you in the form of questions." He sips his new powerful martini, rests his cigar in the ashtray, and raises a thumb of approval in Buddy's direction. "When you are with a woman, does she always come?"

"I don't know."

"You *don't* know? Don't you ask her? Doesn't she tell you? Don't you listen to her breathing? You don't look into her eyes?"

"I do it with my eyes closed."

"You don't feel her body collapse? You don't *know*? You does-be sleeping whilst your're fooping? But for you to say you *don't know* . . ."

"Me and sex was never happily married. To me, it is something like a need."

"But call it what you like," John says, trying once

more with his cigar, "I can't say that every-time that my woman puts that weight on me, that when she rolls off, she is the most *satisfied* woman in the whirl. So, you and me are the same. But if you see what I'm saying, you may not be the only man in this bar this evening that have that kind o' problem. What about the way you does-do it? In the dark? Or with lights on? Do you light candles? Drink wine? Put on soft music? Rub your tongue over her toes? How you does-do it? Are you a bang-bang man? After you tell me, I going-tell you how I operates."

"*That* is what I am talking about. There is something that frightens me about sex. I don't know what is the right time to begin; and sometimes I think she is not ready to begin, and I have to wait for the right moment. I am cat-spraddled beginning-wise and sex-wise, and my tom-pigeon can't make a move. Sometimes the bare idea of having sex scares me. And I feel nervous and start to tremble. And to get it over and conquer my feeling of fright, I want to rush up to her, strip-off all her clothes, muzzle her mouth against any rejection or complaint, and jump-on, and *bang-bang!* Jump off; wash-off myself, put-back-on my clothes, light a cigarette, and slip through the door."

"Goddamn!"

"Sometimes, I hate sex. Really hate sex and find it dirty, physically dirty. Not only from what the Bible says about fornication and covetousness, but normal sex."

"Goddamn!"

"And as we are sitting down here this evening, passing through my mind is all the women, nice women, beautiful women, bright women, intelligent women, women that I have loved, but never told them that I love them. Most of them are dead and I still love them. As I sit down here, drinking with you, I can see each one of them. They all slipped through my fingers. Lost occasions and lost opportunity. And I am left with the feeling of *loss*. Of death. Of loss. Loss."

"Goddamn! And you never sought help?"

"I was never able to talk these things to a woman, and say, 'Darling, I confess that I can't come, and make you happy. So, darling, you could help me to come? Darling, I am a man who can't foop. It is only in my mind, this fooping-thing.' You really expect a man like me to low-rate myself, fall on my two knees in prostration before a woman, and admit my weakness in bed to the *same* woman?"

"Goddamn! Therapy can't help you, brother! Sextherapy can't move you from your position! You're gone, brother, *gone*! A goner for those ideas you just expressed. And you was going-through these things, these afflictions, all these years, and never had anybody, till I came along, to talk-them-over with? Goddamn!"

"You asked me questions about legs and breasts; about feet, teeth, hips, dress, weight, sex and having-sex, colours in a woman's dress and her body, about lingeries and things. It's like holding a book in my hand and reading it. I can't face the pages. I know that this book has-in things I should know. But this book remains *unopened.* Shut tight. Like Klein. I can't open this book at all. Can't dare. Can't get the courage. I am a *lost* case. Lost cause. I feel lost. I am a *lost* case. *Cause.* And I only hope that you would never repeat these things to anybody . . . I wonder, if I had-remained back home, if I would be facing these sex-things, and if these sex-problems are caused by immigrating to Toronto? You have any therapy-books on the subject? But I would only go home to relax and to dead . . ."

The shadows cast by the Tiffany lamps are like kisses on the faces of the men and the women in the bar; and the odour of alcohol and the almost acrid smell of cigarettes, the pungency of John's cigars, sear the eye; and with the film that gathers over the eyes, the light renders the picture of the bar like a painting drawn with watercolours of snow and cloud, mist and vapour. John's cigars come from Cuba. They are illegal in America.

And unknown to us, for we are not paying attention, melodies are being played by a machine that is out of sight, in a corner, perhaps hidden in the lights in the ceiling, or under the carpet under our feet; and this music that has a different character from the one we knew back in those Hit Parade days, seems nevertheless right and proper, in this ticking by of talk and time; and it wraps us, John and me, in a comfort thick as our blood, and we feel we are warm again in the sea water we used to sit in, up to our waists, measuring our safety from the waves that could trick us into deeper adventure, and throw us back again upon the sand, bloated like my uncle's body.

John is talking again. "I miss my thrildren. I miss them real bad, especially at a time like this. The first nine of my ten thrildren I never really seen growing up. But this last one, that's here with me, I intend to be with him *every* day of my goddamn life. I promise him that much." He stops talking and just stares into his glass. Then he says, "You know something? I can go for a year, twelve months, without missing them, and then, *wham!*, at this time, near Christmas, I miss them like hell. I don't miss their mothers. But I do miss my thrildren. Hommany did I tell you I have?"

"Two in France, and three in Italy, and . . ."

"I said I have ten. Nine, plus this one, Rashid, my last, the apple of my old age. I gave him a real African name, purposely. Rashid! I don't really know what it means. But he is Rashid. Every Christmas, wherever they are, they must get in touch with me, and their mothers, too. And every three years it's our reunion-time, when we get together and sit in the backyard round this big picnic table and eat like hogs. My thrildren take after me, food-wise, both the boys and the girls. That's one sure way I know they're all mine, and that their mothers didn't play a . . . didn't *horn* me. From their appetites. And you know something. I always said I prefer to *clothe* them than feed them! But I am glad I have the means to afford these reunions, and to take care of all those thrildren. Did I tell you I have three in France and two in Italy?"

"You said two in France, and three in Italy," I say. There have been so many children mentioned in this long afternoon. "Two in France."

"Your memory is better than mine. I said ten, didn't I?"

"Ten."

"Ten of the best! Nine, plus one."

"But why ten? Why not eight, or nine?"

"Just ten? I wasn't counting whilst I was fooping to have them, if you see what I'm saying."

"But *ten*?" I am thinking how safe I feel, and how safe John feels in this strange place, in this strange bar, with these men and women, none of whom we know, none of whom knows us, and yet their friendliness shines in their smiles each time our eyes meet theirs; and the safety and the comfort and the barman, Buddy from Nova Scotia, are almost like the boys and girls we grew up with, giving me this false sense of safety and comfort, provided by the light from the fake Tiffany lamps; and I continue to feel I am warm again, as if I am on that beach with the sand the colour of the silent pink conch-shell; and I think of the sea and how I measured its cruelty by the drifting in of parts of a fishing boat, and a broken mast and an oar, and I see again the sun turning yellow, or gold, and the green sea changing its roughness in the distance and becoming like an endless sheet of glass that takes in the colour of the sun going down; and I see the broken oar and then a sail, and how it drifts out and out and out into the same waves which bring only death and fishermen's rewards, bloated bodies and dead fish. *Swim-out! Swim-out, man, and get the tire!* "You remember what you told me that afternoon when . . . ?"

"When I told you, swim-out, swim-out, it never had-occurred to me, although in a way I had to know it, that you couldn't swim. How much do you have?"

"Have of what?"

"Thrildren."

"None."

"Even outside-thrildren?"

"None."

"You have an empty life."

"Sometimes, it hits me hard."

"Every man should have *at least* two thrildren. A boy *and* a girl."

"Or five boys and five girls."

"Goddamn!"

"Sometimes, I think I would like to relive my life, and sometimes, I am satisfied; but not always."

"I was an only child, like you was; but I always say I wanted a big family, after seeing all the fun that thrildren of big families in our village had, and even though I didn't plan to have a big family with four women, I still sort-of wanted one, if you see what I'm saying. I sure's hell never *imagine* I would have three wives who wasn't from the Wessindies, and that they would be pure Europeans! I'd be walking down a street and see a man with a black woman, or a black wife, and something would happen to me, something that I can't explain or express in words, if you see what I'm saying; something that I know right here in my guts, but can't put into words. And I feel I would like to place myself in that man's shoes, and try to feel what it is like to be walking down the street beside a black woman, beside a black wife. But I'm destined with a white woman, for a wife. I am gonna tell you something. Where a man lives, so-too does he foop, and so-too does he have to goddamn sleep. If you see what I'm saying. I'll be sixty-three or sixty-five goddamn years old this year, depending on how you look at it, give-or-take a year, and I just emerge from my third divorce. My third, or my fourth divorce? Sometimes, I can't remember the number. Nor the right number o' thrildren that I have. My *fourth*, man. You're looking at a man who been *dee*-vorced four times. Goddamn! Emotionally, I am still reeling from those break-ups. You never get over a dee-vorce. Never. You lie about getting-over it, and pretend you are free. Free at last, free at last! Bullshit! One breaks you up, the second destroys you, and this third cuts you into two pieces. And to go through it four times, goddamn! You're nothing but a quarter of the man you started out as. Your balls're cut into four pieces. All my wives was kind women. Decent women. The fourth wife took me for all I had, or she took me for all she *thought* I had.

But she was still a kind woman. Before her came the Eye-talian opera singer."

"What did she sing?"

"She was Eye-talian, but she wasn't really an opera singer in the sense that she sang operas and arias, like that Southern woman, like Leontyne Price, who, incidentally, lives in the South. Or, Callas. If you see what I'm saying. She wasn't . . . really . . . a singer in that sense. She sang around the house. She sang when she was in the shower. And she was big. You know me and women with weight! But to me. She was an opera singer. I just call her that. I call her the opera singer because of the avoirdupois. To *me*, she was a beautiful woman, like an opera singer. And after this *la-dolce-vita* lady, Dolly or Dolores, I am trying now to make a life with a lady from Durm-North Carolina, a lady by the name of Wilhelmina. Part German. Part Dutch. Part Austrian. Part French. And part Jewish. She tells me this whenever I watch Jesse Jackson and the question of black and white is raised, that her background is German-Dutch-Austrian-French and Jewish, when I tell her mine is black. Goddamn! All those parts! Life just got to be so many goddamn parts, and hyphens, when people can't get together. Come closer. Hold over. Lemme let you in on a secret. Two hundred. And thirty pounds," he whispers. "Two hundred and three-zero pounds . . ."

"Is she here with you? Where's she now?"

"Durm. North Carolina."

"Goddamn!" I say, and he laughs.

"You're beginning to talk like an Amurcan, from the South. Where is she? Well, let's say she's here with me, and she's not here, if you see what I'm saying. In her heart, in her heart of hearts, she's here, but her spirit, her life-force, is back in Durm."

"Her life-force?"

"Morally."

"But, in other words, she's here with you."

"Goddamn! I wish I could say more."

"I don't need to know more."

"How did we get-onto this? My asking you if you have a woman? Or thrildren?"

"Both," I say. "How many children . . . ?"

"From the woman from Durm-North Carolina, I have one child. A boy-child. Who turned out wrong. Named after an African. Rashid. I blame the Amurcan environment. Outta the ten thrildren born to me all over the whirl, to have the tenth turn out like this pisses me off, and saddens me. Make me saddened. But I am not blaming anybody. And I won't blame God. But I axe myself. I axe myself if I have done something wrong. If I been a bad influence or something, having these thrildren and getting divorce, and leaving my thrildren in four parts, quarters. And at *this age*! To be now starting over, with a new slate? You think I been a bad influence? You think I'm begging for trouble? Look me in my goddamn face. And tell me. If, by having ten thrildren, nine straight thrildren from

three legal wives, and this tenth bastard from a'
outside-woman, am I the right role-model for this
goddamn delinquent that I helped to born? Look me
in my face!"

"You have nine-other good ones."

"I have nine others, yes. I have nine others. But this
one is special." He drinks off the martini. He beckons
Buddy over. His fingers are shaking. He takes out his
cigar case, a huge crocodile-leather case, and extracts
a cigar. The label round the cigar says *Monte Cristo*. He
takes the label off, and wears it as if it is a ring, on his
little finger. He takes out his cigar clipper. He clips off
the end and he places the cigar into his mouth. He
passes the match bearing the name of the bar in a slow
circular motion at the tip of the cigar. He makes short,
almost silent puffs on the cigar, and to me it is like the
firing of a gun with a silencer attached to it. The tip
is glaring red. And then, he takes a long draw on the
cigar, holds the smoke in his lungs, savouring its taste
and its power and strength as it goes through his
system, and then he shoots it out. The smoke covers
me and, for a moment, I cannot see the three women
sitting close to our table. His eyes, for that moment, are
hidden from me.

"Don't axe," he says. "I not gonna tell you as much
about this one, the scion of my old age. Goddamn
beautiful boy. But he came out wrong. Me and his
mother aren't married, as I say, but I'm thinking of it,
for goddamn sure! I *love* weddings."

"The fourth hanging."

"For-goddamn-sure! The fourth henging, when I walk up the aisle with this one. Or the fifth? You ever walk-up the aisle? Other than as a choirboy? You say you haven't been married-off, yet?"

"Nope."

"Goddamn. You are a lucky son of a bitch, if you see what I'm saying. How come no Canadian woman haven't hauled your ass up the aisle? How come?" He puffs his cigar, his jaw becomes swollen with smoke and he has the attitude of a man who holds a large cigar in his mouth, and he continues to hold the smoke, and then he jets it out straight into my face; and says, "Wouldn't be AIDS or sickness of that sort, now, would it be? *Naw!* Not at your age! . . . If you see what I'm saying . . ."

"Too busy."

"You don't have confidence in holy matrimony, or what?"

"In money."

"Root of all evil. Not only the root, but from my experiences, the square-root of all evil. The square-root," he says. He is tired. His face becomes a face of thick hanging jowls under his chin. I become concerned that he is aging in front of my eyes. I think of his young wife and his young son. I want to ask him if he is here to get an operation for an old man's disease. But I remember he said Sick Children's Hospital, many times, in reference only. It's the child.

"What is wrong with your son?" I ask him.

"One reason I'm glad I'm here," he says, "apart from the Sick Kids Hospital, is to get me a cashmere topcoat, with the same cut as yours. Stannup. Just for a minute, and let me see how your coat hangs." I stand up, feeling a little stupid. "I can't find me a good tailor in the States. The fashion magazines are turning men into women, if you see what I'm saying."

"Unisex," I say. And I sit down.

"No difference," he says. He is tired, and getting older from the drink.

"Why are you here?" I say. For a while, he does not answer. "For an operation? Prostate? Ulcers?"

"What did you do, when you worked? Were you fired? Injured? Are you in compensation?" he says. And then he says, "Major, something major. With the little one, my tenth child."

I feel stupid, as I did when he asked me to try on my cashmere winter coat, to stand and model it for him. I bought the cashmere winter coat at the Goodwill store. But I will not tell him this. It is my secret, my front, my image of respectability. So, too, will I not tell him why I do not work.

"Doing well?" he asks me. I can feel the fatigue in his voice. "Car? House? Investments?" he says, as I nod my answer to each of his questions. This makes him ask, "Doing so well, and no goddamn wife nor thrildren?"

"Car. House. Few investments . . ."

"Amurcan or European car?"

"Benz. House in Rosedale," I say.

"What's Rosedale? A housing-project? Community-housing?"

"You *could* call it that. Rosedale is sometimes like a community-housing project. I never thought of it that way, but it could be. It is . . ."

"What did you see, when me and you was sitting down, back-there on the beach, wearing our make-believe bathing trunks, some fifty years ago, and looking out into the goddamn sea? What did you see? When you looked out in the sea? What did you see in the sea? What did you really see?"

"Ships."

"Ships? Nothing else?"

"And clouds."

"Ships and clouds?" He says this as if it is the echo to my memory, as if it is an echo, time and place here in this bar going back to that time with no change in the time or in the place, as if there is no alteration, and the bar is the beach; and the way he says it tells me that he too is travelling back over all that time, perhaps not in a ship or in the clouds in a plane, but in something, in some frame of mind, medium, attitude, that has the same dependence upon the wind and the movements of water and waves. I look at him after he has echoed the word *ship* and the word *clouds* and I see him as he was then, and as I was then, as we are, *then.* And then he says, "*I saw three ships come sailing in . . .*"

"*Come sailing in, come sailing in,*" I continue. And we laugh aloud. The three women near to us, in this bar, now almost empty, laugh and smile with us, as strangers smile in exchange of happiness and relief, and safety, in a bar.

"Those two old geezers," one says, loud enough for me to hear.

"What do you think they do?" another asks.

"Priests?"

"Lawyers," the first one says.

"How old you think those two are?" the second one says.

"Not a day past forty-nine," the first one says. She is the one wearing the silver pantyhose.

"*Ship sail?*" John says.

"Sail fast," I say.

"Hommany men on deck?"

"Nine!" I say.

"*One* more! One more than nine, leff-back," he says, "and I'm not telling you much about this one, about him. But that's why I'm here. I been at the Sick Thrildren's Hospital." And he says no more. But the grief, and the deep concern surrounding the hospital and the little boy is on his face. And I do not look into his eyes to stare at it.

The snow is still coming down, as if a white sheet has been drawn against the windows, like the snow falls and shades the figures in the showcases of stores outside along Yonge Street, figures of trees and angels and bells, blocking our vision from the people passing outside, from looking outside, from seeing the whiter darkness. I think of the mock battles we used to play in John's house, games sent to him by his father's brother, who spent all his life in America working on a ship; and when he came off, when he got shore leave, he refused to come home, and jumped ship in America. But he sent toys and pens and shoes which were brogues and brown, and heavy, and which John was not permitted to wear to school as part of his uniform, because of the colour.

"No thrildren, eh?" he asks me. "But I axe you that, already."

"No children. You asked me that three times."

"Goddamn! You got me a little confuse, if you see what I'm saying. Thinking in one part of my mind that you may be bordering on the queer, or something, if you see . . . like I mean, on the homosexual . . . see what I'm saying? Some men, in later life, men your age, sometimes change their preference, if you see what I mean. Happens to women, too. Not that they're really-and-truly switched-off from women, and turn on to men, but they prefer the companionship and the company of men to the company of women. Companionship takes over from sex in later life."

"I don't need a companion," I say; and I give off a laugh, a nervous laugh, which causes him to look more steadily at me, into me, into my thoughts.

"It won't bother me if you *was* one," he says. "Some men are born and some men die without knowing that they are. If they are left-handed, or right-handed. It won't split no difference in our friendship."

"I am not *so*," I say.

"Really?" he says. I am beginning to regret meeting him. I laugh again, and he becomes more serious. He does not laugh. And I wonder why I have to say that I am not homosexual, and why he would think that I am.

"I treats all kinds o' therapies. It's the latest thing, like a fashion. The in-thing in society, men playing they are women. They even make movies about it. But you not queer? No skin off my teeth, you know what I'm saying?" He is not smiling; and the cigar is stuffed into his mouth, between his teeth; and his lips are round, round the cigar, tightly pressing on the cigar; and smoke is coming out, it seems, from his clenched eyes. He looks tough. Menacing. I have never seen him look like this. And it frightens me; and makes me self-conscious, that perhaps, deep down, very deep down, there might be this spectre of evidence to prove his speculation; but what the hell! No! Still, his gaze frightens me; and I try to take my mind off it, and take his mind off the pressing speculation, from what he is thinking, back to his concern about his mysterious son in the Sick Children's Hospital; perhaps, off *anything*; and I say, "I had a woman that I loved very much, once; but she . . ."

"Goddamn!" he says; and his face becomes smooth and warm, and his lips relax, and he looks like a child sucking a large nipple of a feeding-bottle. The tip of the cigar glares and I can smell its strong beautiful aroma.

"It was a bad experience. Once . . ."

"Tell me about it. In my profession, I have to listen to everything."

"She is Chinese."

"You told me about that one, already. But you said she's dead. Didn't you tell me she is dead? In the photograph you showed me?"

"She's not dead."

"You said she was dead. Goddamn. You *sure* you're not talking about the same dead woman? How're you using 'dead'?"

"She is very bright and intelligent. A beautiful woman, lovely in a way. She is a refugee. But before that, in Shanghai, she was a law student; and then she became a law student here. Tiananmen Square?"

"Tiananmen Square was a motherfucker. I saw it on CNN. In Europe, I used to walk-around with my personal copy of Mao's 'Little Red Book'! Saw the whole thing on CNN. But one thing about Chinese women, those Chinese women I hear, are . . ."

"I always become closer to her in September, when the leaves change."

"Didn't Tiananmen Square take place in November?"

"Always in September. The day we met at a bus stop, on Yonge Street, this very street where I also met you, she was . . ."

"Are you *sure* Tiananmen Square didn't take place in November?"

". . . she was wearing a white cotton dress with a yellow scarf round her neck, loose-fitting; you could hardly make out her shape under the dress, but you could see that she had nice calves, the legs of a woman who spends time, lots of time, in dancing, or walking; and I always remember her white dress, that dress I'll always remember coming down to six inches below her knees. That long white cotton dress, with a sash at the back that was not tied. She wore that white dress as if it was her best dress, as if it was the only good dress she had; and I kept thinking, months after I met her, the way she wore that white dress was as if it was made or bought in her home town, and that she was remembering things when she wore it . . . perhaps Tiananmen Square."

"You been *Shanghaied*, brother! You been *took*! *Obsess.*"

"She was taught to do translations in China from Mandarin to English, and she spoke English with an English accent, picked up from listening to the BBC shortwave, a real Oxford-English accent even in China. But why wouldn't she? In China, before she was a law student, she had all her Chinese translated to English; but she didn't finish studying law in China, but here at York University. We met the first time fifteen years ago, when she could have been twenty-one, or thirty-one. I could never tell the difference from her face. This beautiful woman who is so bright has something like a computer-mind, and can talk about anything. After we got close we used to walk from my house all the way to the Chinese market, and all over the city; and although that was a long time ago, fifteen years, this is the woman I am walking to meet and waiting for, and hoping to meet when I walk the streets. After all these years . . . she comes in and out of my life, and in and out of my dreams . . . all the dreams I dream are dreams about this woman."

"Is she goddamn *dead*, or living? I must know. And you must decide. It's an obsession. Chinese women can do that to a man, if you see what I'm saying. What is the name of this Chinese woman that has fucked-up your mind? She *must* have a pretty name, and a prettier body, if you see what I am saying. Names is everything when a man's mind gets fucked-up like this. Names of women. Names of songs that the two o' you listen to, before you was fucked-up. Delilah? Helen of Troy? Cleopatra? How about Chermadene?"

"We used to take trips every Saturday morning to the Allen Botanical Gardens and to all the other places where they grow exotic plants and flowers, and have plants in hothouses, which is one of the things she loves. Used to love. She loves plants, all kinds, tropical plants, equatorial plants, and knows the names of all these plants, can recite them off the top of her head, in English and in their horticultural names; and in her apartment, which I visited only two times, she has three plants in reddish plastic pots. In her small apartment, all the windows are closed, and the three plants are ignored and almost dead. From lack of water and light and plant food, I tell her. No, she says, from love. You can't love a flower in this environment. And the plants can't love you back. She lives in a basement. But does she love plants! In public gardens and city parks and especially in a place out in the suburbs near the Scarborough Bluffs, a hotel with an English name and an English garden which encourages the arts, where artists go, we have walked all these places, to and from. We walk all over the city together, looking for plants and flowers to smell; and one summer afternoon we went to this hotel whose name I cannot remember, and we posed for a picture beside a lion; and then another summer afternoon, I can't remember the year, I was in my backyard in my garden chasing squirrels from my tomatoes and parsley, which they were devouring, and was using my Black Flag on the wood-ants, when the telephone rang. I did not go to the phone immediately, as a line of five big, black wood-ants stuck together were taking my mind off the phone, and I wanted to kill them first before I went to answer the telephone. The top of the can was stuck. I was transfixed by the quin-tuplets of ants, and by the damn squirrels which my neighbour feeds dog food to, on an aluminium pie plate. They were eating my beefsteak tomatoes. I had to squirt the ants dead first, and then shoot the squirrels with Black Flag, and blind the sons-o'-bitches. It was quiet after I killed the ants, and peaceful, and I could hear the leaves blowing; and the two squirrels had vanished. And then I thought of the telephone. It was still ringing; so I walked through the house, through the French doors, took up my Scotch on the way into my study where the telephone is. And then it stopped ringing. The room was suddenly still. I could hear the trees in the backyard blowing. I sat down and tried to remember how many times the telephone rang, was ringing and ringing . . . and ringing . . . and why I thought of the squirrels and the wood-ants . . ."

"And you been here, patient-as-ass, listening to all the crap I been talking, while all the time . . ."

"I never did get up from that chair for hours and hours, thinking of all the calls I have missed in my life. The ice in my Scotch melted, and it turned warm, like soda water with no fizz. And thinking about it now, years later, this thing about time . . . I am always missing time, time is always passing me; so I sat in that chair for hours and hours without moving, just sitting. Hours and hours passed, and I never rose from that chair. That was fifteen years ago. On the ninth of July, to be exact, fifteen years ago. She was too young at the time, even though she was a woman, in mind and body, to be laden with the burden of matrimonial love. So, I was keeping her, keeping her in her virginity for the right day and the right time."

"Keeping her virginity? Is it something for you to keep?" John's eyes widen. I see the confusion in them. And then I see the disappointment. And this turns to disgust. "But, but . . . ," he begins, "but you tell me before that you . . ." His exasperation prevents him from going on. "You even requested divine intervention to help you out!" he continues. "You didn't take it? You didn't take her?" He drops his shoulders, in a gesture of resignation at the mixed messages I had sent him. "You never had sex with this woman? You didn't tell me the exact opposite? When you tell me about getting down on your knees and then ask God for five more minutes when you thought paradise was lost?"

"I was keeping her, keeping her in her virginity for the right time . . . ," I begin to say.

"Fine! Fine, fine!"

"I don't know why. But I had chosen her. She was the one. Fifteen years when I first started to walk this street, Yonge Street, and looking for this woman. And imagine, in all the time I was sitting down in the chair in the study, ants, you wouldn't believe it, wood-ants came out in armies and passed me and passed me, going along on their business, while I am sitting there, after the telephone had stopped ringing hours ago. I was always one for walking every day after I stopped working because of an injury. Just an injury. I sued because I had the injury while at work. I don't like to talk about it, the injury. Suffice to say, it was the kind of injury I could sue for. Not a physical injury. They injured me. They injured me. In a way that never heals . . . But after that telephone call, I started walking the street, day in, day out, religiously, every day, Yonge Street especially, for another reason and for a kind of atonement; and if anybody, anyone out of the thousands of people who see me walking this same street every day, winter and summer, walking this street, without knowing me, they would surely think I am queer or mad, or going off-in-the-head, which may be a point; so, I leave the house down in a ravine not far from where we are sitting now, and walk up the slight incline, and pass the Main Reference Library, that takes me back to those Saturday mornings when we went into Town to the Public Library. And you know something? I never, I have never gone through those doors of the Main Reference Library in this city! I pass it every day. But never enter. Not even to borrow a book. Or look at the pictures on exhibition, and that is a strange thing for a man who back home lived off books. So, I pass the Main Reference Library every day, on Asquith Avenue, turn left on Yonge Street, pass Bloor, pass St. Mary, Wellesley, Gloucester, Wood, College, McGill, Gerrard, Dundas, and on and on, down Yonge Street to the Lake, right down to the Lake . . . I walk those goddamn lonely streets, as you would say; and I stare at the people coming towards me . . ."

"Goddamn! I got it! She lived in Paris! I knew I goddamn knew her! Simone! Nina Simone!"

"Who?"

"The lyrics! The words you just said remind me of a song by Nina Simone! And about your obsession with streets and walking those lonely streets . . ."

". . . and the only thing that happens to me when I walk, the only people that recognize me are people who push little pieces of paper into my hand. I take them and read them when I get back to the house, and I do not throw away any of them; I keep them as bookmarkers, or to write telephone numbers on. One I still carry with me is twelve inches long by five-and-a-quarter, with a large question-mark, the symbol for a question-mark on the front. 'The Most Important Question in the World.' That's the title. Folded in three, and I read the front page, and opened it, hoping to find the answer as I opened each fold, but it gave no answer. It is only a religious tract about death. It does not give me any answers. So, when I had-first-met her, we used to take this same walk; or I would meet her on the way to my house. For the last five years, every day including Sundays, we took the same route; and sometimes, considering the number of Chinese now living in this city, wherever and whenever I take this walk, I see her face recorded in the faces of all the Chinese women I pass. I see her face; and I see more; and I think I see her, and I am on the point of going up to her, to ask her how she is, and apologize about the telephone call, and explain that I did go to answer it, but I didn't answer it in time. Her message was not recorded on the answering-machine, and her face is never recorded in the million faces I meet. And then a message came on the tenth, one day after the ninth of July, fifteen years ago; and I thought it was a joke, that it was a joke, a joke that somebody was playing on me, as how some people change their voices on the telephone, and leave messages about false sadness and false joy, and fear. It was one of those messages that came on the tenth of July. And later in that same week, I am standing over her coffin, and there are flowers all around, for she liked flowers; and five of us – her nephew, his wife, an old woman she rented her first room from, the landlord of her basement apartment, and me – five of us are standing around the rectangle of the hole at which I am looking down, in which is her coffin, with a sprig of the white flower in the pattern of the white dress she first-was-wearing when I met her when I would meet her after work at the same bus stop as the first day. I am standing over her as she lies in her coffin, and I see her in her coffin, I see her face, I see her face every day when I pass Chinese women on Yonge Street; and I see her face every day in my dreams; and it is still a beautiful face, and her hair is still beautiful hair, black silk, long and soft as the fingers of waves that come up and that flow back out along the sand on the beach we used to sit on, and look out into the sea, long as the wave which rolls up along that whole section of the beach, her hair was like a . . ."

"*Don't!*" John says. And straightaway, he says, "Buddy?"

And Buddy comes over and immediately removes the piled ashtray, and Buddy says, "Same again?"

"*No!*" John says. "Two brandies. Best in the house. You got any Spanish brandy?"

"Since that day in July," I continue, "with the sun shining down on the group of us, the five of us, like a punishment more hard than her death itself, and the flowers all around us in vases leaning against other gravestones, in circles of big, thick wreaths; and the little single sprig of white, the flower she liked so much and which I never knew by name, but the sprig of white with deep-green leaves on its branch, all these flowers reminding me it is really a hot summer, a good summer for growing beefsteak tomatoes in the back garden, and for the roses and the geraniums; all these flowers was like if I was back home, and seeing the colours and smelling the colours, and walking in the colours of the hibiscus and the flowers from the cord-ear trees, those white petals, those thick white petals with the touch of pink in the middle. I don't know the names of flowers like she does. But I like to know that there are flowers. And since then, I have no feeling for flowers, or for any other woman; not since then. Not even an occasional woman that a man would invite for companionship or a drink in a bar, or in a restaurant; not even a woman he would invite to his house, if boredom comes over him; not even a woman to visit and look at, knowing that I am not really interested in anyone but her; not even in going with a woman, once in a blue moon. It is like I am going through a kind of religious transformation, a con-version. I mentioned atonement before. I remember in Scripture classes at Combermere School for Boys, they taught us about Paul heading for Damascus, and how the sudden power of conversion was like a stroke of blindness, blinding him to all the other activities going-on round him; and at the same time, it was like a stroke of sight. Things around me, like the Main Reference Library, which they say is the best in Canada, I am blinded to. Like the yearly parade when West Indians dance in the streets. Like the baseball games. And the parties on weekends, and dancing to calypso music on Friday nights at Cutty's Hideaway on the Danforth. Like the presence of other women, like the one who would cook such lovely steaks that were always with too much blood in them, and after dinner continue drinking white wine, and would wear the white, see-through shortie-nighties. Nothing. Nothing comes after that. Nothing after that has any meaning to me. It is like being "saved," when the pastor of the Nazarene Church pushes your head down under the water, and the water gets into your eyes, and the saltiness of the water gets into your mouth and your ears and leaves a white line round your forehead, from the salt in the sea water; and when you come back up, you are not the same person who was buried below the surface of the sea. This woman. This woman, this Chinese woman. She gave me a seal once, that she brought back from China when she visited her father who was dying, made-outta something that looks like marble, of a rich, dark, silver colour, almost like the colour of the pantyhose you liked that that woman is wearing. She had it made specially by a craftsman in China, in Beijing, with a small white animal on the top of the seal. The animal is reclining. I don't remember what she said is the name of the animal, but I remember that the animal in question is the animal after which the year, the year she visited her father, was named, the year she gave me the seal. It is in a box. Rectangular, with silk of the same dark, silver colour, with flowers in the pattern; and the thing that keeps the box closed, its clasp, is a piece of ivory, like a tooth from some other animal, or from the same animal. This oblong box that is a rectangle, and that has a lining of deep-red silk, with an indentation in the middle, for the seal to fit it and rest in and not shake. From that day in the summer, when I didn't answer the telephone, and all these days when I am not walking on the street just outside there from where we are now sitting, I sit and look at this seal and the box it comes in; and I mark the seal on pieces of paper, and on envelopes, and on stationery, and I write letters to her, and seal them, and put them in a drawer, and keep them, and leave them there in the drawer which has dried petals of red roses in it. In winter, when the snow remains for weeks on the black-and-white ground, and when it makes walking impossible and dangerous, I open the letters I write to her, and read them, and fold-them-back and seal-them-back with the seal she brought from China, the seal that has Chinese characters written on it. The red blotter containing the ink on which I have to place the seal is red too, and it is covered with a piece of material, a circular piece of material she cut, careful, slow and with love, with a small pair of nail scissors she would use to clip her fingernails and the excess, long hairs between her thighs; and with this scissors she cut a piece of cloth from a pair of the panties she liked to wear, and . . . had just taken off, to bind me . . ."

"Goddamn!" John taps his Monte Cristo on the edge of the cleaned ashtray and looks me straight in the eye, shaking his head all the time he does this, in compassion, in understanding, in consolation, and at the same time, in shock. "And I been shooting-off my mouth all this goddamn time? And you *let* me?" He taps the cigar again and again, and then places it beside the ashtray, as if he is disregarding it. "I got something to confess to you, when you finish."

Buddy brings the snifters of Spanish brandy; and John lights a match, and applies it to one of the snifters which he then places in front of me. And he does the same thing, with another match, to his own glass, warming the glass. I drink mine off in one gulp. The sting of the brandy is like a sword going through my belly; like the sudden spasm of recollection and of pain I suffer each time I walk out onto Yonge Street, and see a face that is Chinese and a body that is like a young willow sapling, vulnerable and strong and bending to the motion of her legs and arms, a woman with *her* face wearing a white cotton dress that is loose-fitting and with a band that is loosened and untied; and this sharp, painful plunge of remembering makes me sick, makes me want to stop beside a building and bring up the sadness in the telephone call a day after I had not answered the phone, remembering the loss of those days with the flowers we used to stoop to see and sniff in parks and public gardens, and the neglect of her soft youthfulness of truth and of love. She likes to stand on my shoes and have me move about the room, bearing her on them, as if she is a little child, learning the first steps of waltzing from her father. "I love to stand on your feet. It makes me taller; and I feel stronger," she says. I heard her voice that first confessing time and it made me younger; and I hear her voice each time I stoop to put on my socks; each time I stoop a second time to tie my laces; each time I take the seven steps down from my front door to the street. All I have now is the reflection of the roundness of her face and her eyes; and the slow start of her smile which never leaves her lips afterwards; and the imprint of her small feet on my shoes. The imprint of the red Chinese characters sealing my name to her love and to the envelopes that hold the words of love she never got to read. And the seal in the box, lined in red silk. When I returned from looking down into the grave the same in dimensions, but on a larger scale, to the box that contains the seal, and when I take up this box these nights to remember her, I am looking into the same space of the grave, of the coffin, the same space which holds her small, tightened body, formed like a slice of a moon, her back towards me, her hand between her legs, her other hand, in a kind of double-jointedness, planted and printed on my thigh.

"And after all these years!" says John.

"Time draws her closer to me."

"That is real love. One time, and forever. Like my marriages which didn't work out that way. Once and forever. Goddamn."

"This is why I say I have no woman and no child and no love. I do nothing. I am nothing. I feel I am nothing. I feel nothing. Not only in winter when the feeling has to be slightly less cold than the snow. But forever. I have no feeling, no more. Only the feeling of seeing her memory and her face on the faces of the thousands of other Chinese I pass every day and do not know and do not speak to, but watch to see if that same miracle of meeting her will repeat itself in the echo of her voice, and bring her back from the grave . . ."

"One love. Goddamn! One goddamn, short love that is forever . . ."

"The only love."

"I don't feel good after listening to you. After listening to you, I feel like a, like . . ."

"When I reach the Lake these days, and look into the Lake, the water is not as clear like silver as it is on a beach, where . . ."

"Like shit. I feel like shit. Me, reeling-off a lotta goddamn bullshit, and coming-on strong, and behaving like a real goddamn bragging, ugly fucking Amurcan, when you, my ace-boon, my friend . . . You *are* my goddamn friend, you see what I'm saying? The only friend I have ever had, ever will have, brother!"

"Down by the Lake these days, I look into the water and I see nothing. Nothing. Not even my reflection. And one morning, not too long ago, I am looking into the water by the Lake, standing at the railing beside a ship that doesn't sail any more, a ship that is now used as a restaurant serving seafood; and that morning I was looking, I am looking into the water and I see her face. And I moved, immediately, straightaway, because I know if I did not move from looking into that dark, green, dirty water, I would have followed the mirage of her face, and jumped in to meet her."

"Goddamn!" He takes his brandy glass in his right hand, with the cigar still unlit and in the same hand, and he raises it to his lips, lets it touch his lips, and removes it, holding it a few inches from the top of the shiny, round table, and does not taste it. "I got something to confess, my friend." And I wait, and he does not say anything for a while. My mind is on the small patch of bright green mowed grass around the plot where we gathered in the small circle of friends, five that she and I could count, with the brown coffin in the narrow width of the grave, and I am still looking into the small rectangular box covered in dark, silver silk with the red interior lining, looking at the marble seal; at the small body which I cannot see, but which I see clearly; and at the sprig of white flowers with the green branch and leaves; at the body and at the marble seal; and as I am there standing on that grass in summer, John is sitting beside me in this bar, telling me things I hear only in the spaces left over from that memory of that afternoon in the Mount Pleasant Cemetery and Crematorium . . . "I was never married in France, and never had a wife in France . . . and I never had any children from the *parlez-vous* woman," they were not his children, they were hers, from a previous marriage, but he liked them and called them his . . . and I see *her* eating with two long sticks of ivory, and wonder at her dexterity, but I know she is double-jointed for the way she can lie on her left side, and protect herself with the left hand placed between her thighs that are soft, so soft, her thighs that are like two rebellions of passion and feeling when I touch them; and she still has one hand left over for me, to comfort me, to print her five fingers of trust on my left thigh. ". . . is, and was, no wife either in Germany, because I hated Hitler too much during the Second World War, and because my new spouse has Jewish blood among the four other strains in her veins. I could never think of marrying a German woman, even though one presented herself before the other." He is saying that he visited Italy once, and that was for a weekend from England where he was at university, to play soccer, and that his team was drenched six-nil; so, they turned around and drenched themselves in red wine from the Caves of Barolo . . . "I was living with the *frauleene-woman*, and, like the first woman, she has the thrildren, who became my step-thrildren . . ."; I am still standing over her, as they pour the dark-brown mould, thick as molasses, crumbling and pouring over her small, stiff body, over her soft olive skin, in too plentiful, too hasty, too unspeakably large shovelsful, as if they want to make sure she will be buried forever, and is nourished well by this thick layer of earth, to grow beneath the earth like the plants and flowers she loves. John is still talking: ". . . and I don't know why I would tell you all that bullshit, as if I wanted, as if I had to impress you, you who I haven't lighted an eye on, in all these years. It's pure bullshit! In my profession, I know what this means. But . . ."; and I am standing in her small apartment in a basement owned by the Italian construction worker, her land-lord, who enters her room after his wife has gone to bed, through the unsealed door beside the furnace which he has never fixed, bending his head under the uncovered pipes of hot water, cold water, and sewage, to stand in the darkness, which is frightening, and ask her if there is anything she needs, and who remains even after she has sworn three times that she is "fine, fine, fine"; I stand in this small one-room apartment watching her three plants that need love and water and some light, watching her cook a meal in four parts using a single pan that looks like a large version of the ink-pad for my seal, a wok; and I watch her dexterity as she keeps hot the previous three cooked courses of the four-pronged meal she learned in China; and how she is able to serve them, piping hot, to suit my peculiarity, even though in the menu of her ancient land and culture, cold was the order of the night; ". . . but I'll tell you the truth. The truth is that I came up from Durm-North Carolina by train, and that my boy is in the hospital, over there somewhere, somewhere from here, at the Sick Thrildren's Hospital, under annastettics, waiting for the doctor to operate, waiting for an operation that may take his goddamn life, or that may save his life, I don't know which; and the child's mother is at the hospital now, 'cause I left her there as I couldn't bear no more to look at my goddamn child strapped up to all those goddamn tubes and with a machine beating in place of his heart, and suffering so much pain, that little bugger in all that pain and suffering. We're supposed to leave tomorrow, if everything goes according. Anytime now, or later tonight, he would have come out from under the surgeon's knife . . ."; and the second time I arrived at the apartment, she made me ring the bell four times, and knock five times, and she remained at the door until I had done that, and then she answered the door, with a loud welcome, "Come in, come in, come in," because she wanted me to make noise and announce my presence in full hearing of the landlord, and put him on notice, in case he was lurking in the furnace room. She wanted him to know she had chosen me for her bed. And when I entered, she called out my name, three times, aloud, and later she told me in a whisper that this precaution was her protection from the nightly visits of her landlord; to ward him off . . . ; " . . . the truth of the matter is that I live in Durm-North Carolina, and I really work in a firm of social workers, but I do not do all the things I told you I do, all that, some o' that is bullshit, if you see what I'm saying . . . It's a damn job, that much is true. I'm the manager of the office, but I try my hand at some therapy and counselling, when the real medical and psychology staff are not present. It's my way of learning things, and helping with my studies at college, where I go every night after work and on weekends, to improve myself . . ."; and on that first night, we watch television in black and white on the two channels she gets, and talk about all the languages they speak in China; and how she learned to speak such good English from the BBC International Service; and about Barbados which she has read about in books in school in China; and about the first night she arrived at the airport in Toronto here, frightened by the English language which she could not follow because of its Canadian accent and the Immigration officer who did not speak English with the same BBC accent as hers. She knew what he was saying to her, but still could not understand his English under the glare of the fluorescent questioning, and the people who spoke it in such loud insistence, enunciating each slight syllable and prejudice, stressing each suspicion and disapproval of her immigrant presence. That night, I knew that I loved her, because she and I were so close . . . and we fell asleep at four in the morning, my head to her feet, at opposite ends of the small creaking bed that had no blanket to clothe her against the cold, against the lowered heat from the landlord's spitefulness and economy, from the vengeance of his unrequited visits.

The snow has now completely cut us off from the sidewalk and the street outside. There are only six of us left in the bar, the three women who are now silent, fixing their lips with Zilactin in preparation for the searing coldness of the wind that howls at the sealed windows, that pushes against the bolted front doors. Only the three women, and Buddy and John and me. Buddy is polishing the washed glasses, and moving a bottle of liquor one inch in one direction, and then another inch in the opposite direction, for symmetry, or perhaps according to the percentage of proof in the alcohol in the bottles; and as he does this, the two waves of bottles are reflected in the long mirror in front of which they stand, closer now, coming in an unending line like a wave of snow left by the snowplough against the length of the gutter. He is not satisfied with his arrangement, and changes the symmetry, moving one bottle closer to another, and moving it back an inch, until the geometry in his mind is mirrored by the running line of bottles of all shapes and sizes and contents. The music is no longer playing. But we do not miss it. It must have been buried in our conversation and then was unnecessary, and Buddy turned it off. The music passed away without notice, just as the other customers have left without a farewell. The bar is quiet. And we can hear only the noise of passing cars, the sound of slush and some skids caused by sudden acceleration over ice, like the waves that used to lap over our feet, then speed back to the sea, leaving us sitting in the sun on the sand, beside the old conch-shell the fishermen used to summon villagers for their catch, and summon villagers to a death by drowning of a fisherman.

"I hope you didn't get the impression while I was talking all that bullshit," John says, "that I was suggesting there was anything wrong with you, if you see what I'm saying. It's been a long day. And we had a lotta catching-up to do, but I didn't mean to come on strong, and suggest there is anything psychologically wrong with you, and that I was making myself a role-model for you. Shit, I isn't a role-model even for myself!"

"I took it serious, but I didn't take it so."

"'Cause we grew up together. And what happened to me happened to you. What is wrong with me is wrong with you."

"From small. We were always together."

"And we goddamn know each other, from the time when you even couldn't swim. Library, school, playing cricket and football, Lilliputian-cricket kneeling on our knees in the broad-road and batting, and marble-cricket; running all over the goddamn pasture playing we are athletes and sprinters . . . goddamn! My life is your life, your life is my life, my life matches your life. So, for me to come-on strong, as I did, I musta-been out o' my *goddamn* mind! We went to the Public Library every Saturday to get books to read in reading-races between me and you, goddamn, man, what got into me to . . . if you see what I'm saying . . ."

"It never crossed my mind. Seeing you and chatting with you has helped to make me forget time and forget the terrible, sad life I have been having here. It made me forget. I have forgotten, for the time we were sitting drinking, that I wanted to go back to the house. And it saved me from having to enter an empty house, once more. Sometimes, it feels like a house with a ghost in it, although I don't believe in such things. It has a ghost, or a curse, in it. Seeing you has-brought-me-back to life. If you see what I'm saying."

"I see where you're coming from."

"Closing-time," John says. "Closing-time, now."

"*Past* closing-time!" Buddy says, glancing behind, still polishing glasses, and moving bottles of liquor, one closer to the other, and then changing his mind.

"Time to close," John says.

"Closing-time!" Buddy says.

"What're we doing here, still?" one of the three women says; and together they rise, and run their hands over their waists, over their hips, ironing out the creases and the hours from their sitting. Their faces are ready now for the sharp bite of the night; and their winter coats are on their bodies, and their bodies have grown suddenly larger under the wool, and still they shake their bodies in a playful jerking, anticipating the sudden fall in mood and the change in the temperature. "We

should all be in the Caribbean, laying on some beach!"
one says. We hear her.

"That's for goddamn sure!" Buddy says, liberal and
expressive in his comments, now that the bar is closed.
"That's for sure! This *cold*?" And he too shakes his
shoulders, as if he is shaking snow from the collar of
his winter coat.

"'Night!" the women say, in three voices, at three dif-
ferent times, one after the other, almost in unison in
their enjoyment.

"'Night, guys!" one of them says, speaking for the
other two. And they leave. They leave as they had
entered hours earlier, showing no effect from the long
night, with no alarm and notice, just three women
walking in out of the afternoon cold to get warmer, to
have a drink to make them feel warmer, and walking
out now.

"You ladies get home safe, now!" Buddy says. "Drive
carefully!" And all three of them wave their gloved
hands over their heads without looking back, and
giggle a little, and before the doors are closed behind
them, we can hear the exclamation from their mouths,
telling us how much colder it has become outside on
the dead street. The slush raised by a passing car is like
the sound of waves beating against a breakwater.

John sits for a while, not talking, just running his
fingers round and round an expensive unlit cigar, fol-
lowing the flashes of his face reflected in the mirror
behind the bottles of liquor on the shelf; and Buddy,

fussing like a housewife, moves one bottle a short distance, and puts it back in its former spot, as if he is killing time.

"Family?" John asks him.

"Wife and three kids," Buddy says. "Lovely family. I'm going home to a warm bed, a lovely woman, and who knows what else! Who *knows* what else, eh?" He laughs, telling us by his laugh that we know what else. "Yeah, I'm a family-man."

"Goddamn lucky!" John says.

"Been watching you two fellas all night. You sure are tight. Good friends. From out of town? Good to see old friends get on like you two. Me, I have a friend like that. Left him back in Sydney-Nova Scotia. He wouldn't leave Sydney. Even with all the unemployment in Sydney, he never wants to leave. Buried him last November, never wanted to leave Sydney, left only once to come to visit me and take in a Blue Jays game while he was here, but never left Sydney after that. But what a guy!" And he moves from behind the bar, and he is carrying two large snifters of Spanish brandy poured up to the thick fat belly of the glass, and without another word puts them down before us. He is back behind the bar, and he says, "On me, take your time. I have a few more minutes to check things. Take your time, take your time. Cheers!"

I lift my glass, and the action takes my eyes to John whose face is lined with tears that stop at the fatness of his cheeks; and I think of that one finger of sea water, a stranded wave, which comes up too far onto the beach and dies in the sand at my feet, and I watch it die, and do nothing about its separation from the rest of its family of waves.

"We leave the cradle," John says, "and our mothers who bring us into this whirl, who bring us up, on Cream of Wheat, and feed us food to make us into men; and we leave them behind and we take our different paths in different directions in different countries that we know about only from books we read in school, countries we make our beds in, and we never get the chance to go back to the place where we were borned, and we never grow up really, 'cause we leave the only place we know, too early, too young; and we leave the island as forced-ripe men, and we never get real ripe, or grow up. Goddamn! We leave the cradle where we know everything about it, the marks we put there as little thrildren with our teeth, the stains from peeing in it, the holes in the mattress from standing up in it, looking out through the bars in it, seeing things through those bars around us that don't harm us, things that love us. But leaving that cradle so early, leaving that nest, that bed, and coming away, we never grow up into men, really. And it take me all the travelling I been travelling, coping, copping a plea, getting into trouble which I didn't tell you about, shifting, slipping punches and landing a few myself, all these things only for a goddamn man to be able to say he's a man; and the punches that I throw are only a few, only a goddamn few for a man of my learning and education.

It take me all that travel I been travelling to understann that years and time can't change a man, can't change how we, you and me, start-out on a beach, two barefoot boys looking into the goddamn sea and seeing things, things which we didn't even know we was watching and seeing. Sometimes, when I think of those times, at my desk in the office of the social services place where I am the supervisor, right there in Durm, North Carolina, sommany miles from that island, sometimes, at those times, I tell myself that we shouldn't have-look so goddamn hard. That we shouldn't have-had the means o' seeing. Because, perhaps, if we didn't look so hard, spraining our eyes and making our eyes water from the concentration, and the glare off the sea, we would still be on that beach, happy and innocent. Still sitting on the sand, looking out at the ships and the fishing boats that bring-in the tourisses and visitors and fish. Certainly we won't be in all this fucking cold!" John shakes his shoulders, pretending he is freezing. And then, he just sits, and does not say a word, and does not move. His silence is heavy. I cannot bear it. I feel he has spoken his part, and the silence that has dropped I take as my cue to travel in my own thoughts.

So, I sit at the house in a chair, and wait for that telephone call to come a second time even though I know it won't; and I sit for all hours of the night, one, two, sometimes up to three in the morning, waiting; and I know that this time I shall rush to answer it, and I will have to answer it; but I also know now that it will never ring a second time, not like the first unanswered time on that summer day when I was in the garden at the back, chasing squirrels and killing wood-ants with my Black Flag. A grown man, sitting fully dressed, with shoes on, in a chair, holding a can of Black Flag, an extra-large size, waiting and wondering why my life would want to smother me in an empty haunted house in Rosedale.

"When Lang passed away," I say, "when she died, the first thing that came, the first thing that came into my mind was the old conch-shell lying on the beach. I wonder who blows it, now? Lang has the same colour almost – had – and it is strange that I would compare the colour of a conch-shell, especially the colour of the conch-shell in early summer, to the complexion of Lang. I think about that, all the time, the colour of her skin and the colour of our conch-shell. I have left the beach, and exchanged it for Rosedale, living in a big house of wood and glass and concrete and wood-ants, and empty. Me, in this house, with nothing to do but sit and wait, sit and take my daily walks because I can't do anything else, not since the injury. Retired through injury before I reached retirement age, with all the things a man craves. Except one. Except that one person. So Rosedale means nothing now that she is only a ghost, my ghost in the house I live in. Rosedale is nothing like that day on the beach, sitting on the sand beside you. Sometimes, I ask myself why couldn't I see on that day, and at that time, as clear as

I see the marble seal in the silk silver-grey box she gave me. Why in my youth I could not see that I would meet this woman, this Lang, and have happiness as long as the moving waves; and why did my happiness last only for two or three months, the late summer and the first chilly months of fall, for such a short space of time. This loss, the loss of Lang, is a long way to travel to, a long way to go, a very long way and time, for such short happiness."

"Let's go. Let's close the joint."

"It is closed, John."

"Goddamn!"

"What's the time, now?"

"Time?"

"Night-time."

"Twelve, yet?"

"One gone!"

"Let's go. There's nothing left."

"There's nothing waiting."

"Let's go."

"Yeah! Let's get to-hell outta here!"

The snow outside the front doors is like a single step I have to step up on, and then straddle to reach the sidewalk which has disappeared in the long, unblemished, bodiless whiteness. The marks I leave, no smaller than the marks he leaves, go down deep into the fresh foam, and in the night. The dampness bathes our feet and washes the leather of our shoes in a kind of chill caused by a fever. We stand a little outside the black doors, catching our breath which spurts out in bursting vapours like from the nostrils of some fire-breathing animal.

"This shit," John says, "I walked through this shit in Paris, Berlin, in Brooklyn, and now *here!*"

We catch our composure and our balance, and we move on, in some direction. The night is quiet and cold and we are the only two persons in this sleeping street, except for the dead mannequins raised by the winking lights in store display windows, and the lazy traffic lights changing from red to yellow to green. I pull my collar up to my ears, and still I feel razors of cold steel puncturing my face. "This *shit!*" is all John says about the cold that is walking through my body and through his.

"I am damn scared to go back," he says, and he spits into the fresh, unspoiled snow. The brown blob slaps the snow and spreads and then disappears under the whiteness, leaving only a smudge, some kind of indication of the fear that grows within him, the fear to face the truth, to face the hospital, to face his son, to face his woman. "I am not a brave man, Timmy. I never was a brave man, even when I had the cobblers in my foot, and I axed you to swim-out for that goddamn rubber tire. I knew all the time that you couldn't swim. I had to know. Things like this you have to know, just as I know my weakness after years of pretending that I am a brave son of a bitch. Some of the things I tell you back there was true. Some was true. It don't matter now which o' them was true. But some is true, bound to be, if you see what I'm saying."

"I am not going to take you home. To my house."

"I didn't axe."

"Not because of anything. I am not taking you to my house. No one, no one but me enters that door. Not since Lang. The week after, I got rid of the house-keeper. Now I think the house is suitable only for her ghost, her presence. Her presence in her absence. Sometimes, I don't shovel the snow, or take out the garbage. My Christmas tree is still up. From three Christmases. It is just a place. A big, beautiful place, though. But not happy. Walking this street, Yonge, much earlier in the year, I would walk-back-down into the ravine, and instead of going inside, right away, like a normal man going home, I would sit in the front garden, on the wrought-iron bench there, and look at the flowers, and follow the marching of those wood-ants, and become so tired from looking at them, and so disinterested that I won't raise a finger sometimes to squirt them dead with my Black Flag. In the winter-time, like now, I would remain in the front garden, and sit and sit and sit, ignoring the cold iron bench, and look at the dried, dead flowers which is all she left, the flowers and what the flowers mean. The flowers in this city are different. Have you noticed? There are differ-ent flowers here, not like the ones back home; but they are *her* flowers, Lang's flowers. When you carry a woman out of your house, your home, and you bear her to another place to rest, you can't easily take another woman through those same doors. Or a friend, even. Not if you have a heart."

"Your mother always said that. 'If you have a heart.' If you have a heart, you would never think of doing this, or doing that. If you have a heart. I now know what she meant when she said it. If you have a goddamn heart! I-myself can't go back to that hospital. I don't have the heart to do it. I can't face much more in my life, 'cause I don't have the fucking heart, and I never was a brave man. But I have to."

"You have the time?" I ask him.

"Time?"

"What is the time?"

"I should be getting back to the hospital."

"It's night-time."

"Twelve, yet? I'll get back though, and sit in the Emergency, till a nurse tells me where to go, to the waiting room, or some place . . . near his room, and wait. I was in the corridor outside his room and I got up and just walked out. Just walked out because I couldn't face it no more; so, I took a stroll and end-up bumping into you, and imagine . . ."

"Winter makes time look the *same* time, whatever is the time!"

"Look at this *shit!*"

"When I had to go to work before my injury, it was this time of the year that took the life outta me; leaving in the darkness, working in the darkness, although there were fluorescent lights, and returning to the house in the dark, in darkness, even though the snow is white. I call it, this time o' year, the white darkness, the white darkness."

And we walk slowly because of our age, and also because we are more accustomed to walking through sea water and wet sand, and also because of our tipsiness. Like two fishing boats without sails, rudderless in the broiling white foam of the waves. We walk with our arms round each other, affection and guidance, ballast we always found in our lives; two old black men coming through a storm in a place we do not really know.

"It's safer here, though," John says, reading my thoughts.

"Safer than the South?" I ask nevertheless.

"If this was Durm . . . ," he begins, and says no more.

"I'll walk you to Sick Kids," I say, protectively.

"No, you won't. I can find my goddamn way in any storm! This ain't the worst shit I have walk-through, brother!"

I know where we are walking, I know what we are passing. I know the names of the stores and the names of the streets, and I know that after all these years of walking, I am still passing these same strange monuments that bear no relation to me, and I know even in this thickening snow that they mean nothing to me, because they do not know me. That I can pass this stretch of road, black in warm weather, and white in winter, and go alone with my thoughts down to the

Lake and stand and lean and give the impression that the Lake is calling me into its dark, dirty, oily green water that is pulling me to her face, which I can see on its unmoving looking-glass. And no one would raise a hand, lift a finger until afterwards, after the body has splashed into the thick, oily green, after the stench rises to mark the difference. And I can walk these streets in a darkness of unrecognition, and only the store windows and the unseeing mannequins inside them would know I have seen them. Look now. Here. They sell records here, reggae and dancehall and calypsos; and beside it they sell classical records at bargain prices; here, they sell jeans and in the summer the jeans are made easier to be purchased by the blaring music from the tropical part of the world, funky, raw, pulsing and passionate and scary. And when it is time for the body to drink in its tonic of heat and barbecues, they sell T-shirts with names from all over the world, designers' names, political slogan names; and beside the stall that stands like a tired sentry-man in summer there is a stench of pee from the men without homes who make a bathroom of the wall and of the short, hidden, safe alley adjacent. And across the street is the Eaton Centre, now like a grave; in the daytime filled with flowers and smells and people. And this street. Running silently at this time of day or night, at this ungodly hour, this street, Dundas Street, a vein that pumps people into the section of this city that I like best, into Chinatown where she fades and becomes buried amongst the hundreds of other faces from China, where she and I eat the entrails of pig and chicken and duck, with two long sticks made out of fake ivory. This street corner is where my breath leaves me each time I reach it. It is here that her body comes pelting back to me in various positions and times, when I feel the presence of her love in a fast, short thrust of passion and affection, something they call emotion. Thick and raw and smelling fresh and still moving, like the blood of the pig stuck under the neck. I must face the truth on this street. I must face the truth of this street. Our short, thick life together was never consummated. It was just a touch, an intention . . . Here, right here, is the street, Dundas Street and Yonge, the intersection where my feet pull me every day of my walking, as they pull me now, as I am walking beside the best friend I have left in this world. But the world is getting whiter and colder and, at the same time, black with danger, for if a policeman should see us, obvious and standing-out on this landscape this time of Michaelmas and Good King Wenceslas, in this silent night, and if he is in the wrong frame of detectiveness, we do not have to be in Durm, North Carolina, or on Utica Avenue, Eastern Parkway, or Nostrand Avenue in Brooklyn, for him to "pull us over," even though the only carriage is our feet. Our feet are our only carriage, somebody else said.

"The cold sure as hell brings life into your body! A strange thing! The cold make me feel sober. They say it makes you look younger. You look more younger than me. I be living in all that heat in Durm, and you living in all this goddamn cold, walking through all this shit!"

We stand over a round hole in the white pavement, marked out clearly through the difference in temperature, and we feel warmer; our feet are two temperatures as if they are melting minute by minute. As we stand a policeman in a cruiser the same colour as the snow passes his eye over us, and continues on his way. John makes a slight jerk with his body, paying sudden attention. "The Man," he says, softer than he needs to, for the window of the cruiser is closed against the cold. "The motherfucking *Man*, y'all!" and I feel and share the glee in his voice which shivers from the cold. We stand over the round iron hole and watch the steam rise; and we like this warmth, and we do not move immediately. And just like that, in the warm white night, our affection for each other comes to the top and we are hugging and slapping one another on the back and turning round and round and slapping as we turn; and shouting and laughing. The snow falling around us takes our voices, and magnifies our exhilaration, as we dance and turn. And then fall, still clutching each other, in the warm thick snow. It was just like this when the last wave, that last time at Paynes Bay, carried us, sitting in the inner tube, up onto the wet beach.

"Try one of my cigars," John says. We are still sitting up in the snow. "They're good for you, but don't tell the Surgeon General I say so!"

The burning brown cylinder warms my hand, and the strong smell, the smell of success and of confidence, takes me on the swirling smoke to the dining room of Trinity College, where old men with paste in their complexion and thin strands of silver in their hair, eat. I imitate them, dressed in old tweed jackets with patches of leather or suede on their elbows, for economy and category, and follow their mannerisms as they lift their heavy brown pieces of rolled tobacco to their lips, ponderous and bulging, in the middle of their small round mouths. They look like babies feeding from a bottle. I move my cigar as they do, scotched at the sides of their mouths, showing the teeth, showing the accumulation of spittle, and speaking words covered in the richness of dark-brown sherry and port.

"I will walk you to the hospital," I tell him.

"I have to face this alone. I am scared. But lemme *try* to face this alone."

"I wish I didn't make, I didn't allow my house to be turned into . . . to take on the ambience of a tomb . . . I'm not saying this too well."

"No problem," John says. "I know."

"It is not a place to take anybody any more, not since I carried her body . . ."

"I am sorry."

"I am sorry that . . ."

"Who axed you to swim-out? Eh? Who was sitting on the goddamn wet sand on the beach with me that evening when the cobbler got-in my foot? Eh? Who?"

"Me."

"Well?" he says. "*Adios!*"

I am standing alone over the breathing manhole, looking at his cashmere winter coat as it becomes indistinguishable from the falling snow out of the skies I can never see in winter, as he is being swallowed up, devoured in the glistening night, which like a contradiction is dark; and in this puzzling light in which I have lived for more than fifty years, I watch that part of my life slip into the unmarked snow that a man not accustomed to walking in can disappear in. The snow is blowing in a wind, and the smokescreen buries him from my view, as if he was never here, never beside me. I feel angry at this snow, at this wind and this cold. It is like razors slicing my face and my legs. They say that the winter preserved the carton of milk for days and days, for longer than if it was left in the heat. The snow has buried him from my view, from my arms, and I am cold and angry at the murder it has just committed. My face is getting frozen. There are tears on my face. From the circle of land on which I am standing, and feeling the small warmth of the circle I am standing on, like the small island in which I was born. The longer I stand on this iron circle, the sooner I know I have to abandon it, get off and continue into this late night. I do not even know where I want to go. Which direction? And to what destination? The more I stand, the greater is the urge and the knowledge that I must step off from its temporary warmth and walk and walk, continuing in the direction I am taking, away from the house in which I live.

After a while I am closer to the Lake, standing unsteadily at this street corner, Yonge and Queen, with the sidewalk slipping underneath my feet as if the street is melting, is the intersection that it takes courage to cross. And when crossed, it changes my life, and empties me into a cinema from the wrong end, the end that holds the screen and the moving figures, and gives an inverted version of things and faces and people. She was standing here, debating her own crossing, whether to walk with the green and wait for the other green, or wait longer and continue her walking on the same side. I was on the opposite side, with no reason to run the lights; and she changed her mind and waited; and we crossed this intersection together; and did not speak until we stepped off on the other side. She spoke and I answered her question; but I cannot remember her question now; and before she went on her job interview to be an interpreter of foreign languages, we sat in the small coffee shop in a vast basement shopping mall, and she drank her coffee and I watched mine grow cold and unappetizing. And like that she was a part of me. Love was born in that crowded, clattering place of numerous round tables and plastic cups and spoons.

There is a bus stop at this corner. But neither she nor I was waiting for its transportation. So, here I am now, at this intersection, seeing her as she was dressed in the loose-fitting white dress with the band not tied, hanging from her back; here as if I expect she will rise up from the white carpet that covers her grave; here I am remembering the Saturday afternoon we went on the long journey by streetcar and two buses to reach the suburbs, so that she might look at the flowers of the gardens of the Guildwood Inn, and sit on a rock beside the water which has no sand, and toss smaller rocks into the unmoving water. The street is empty now, and I can hear the squeaking of the snow under my shoes, slow for safety and balance and leading me to the point in this walk where I go every day, every year since she died, but never at this hour. And I pass things and places which I paid no attention to on previous walks, but now, I can feel the warmth from the round iron grate, and my body once more has the life of summer. The street is empty. I can hear voices of men and women, and hear their footsteps and see their smiles as they carry bags and boxes and parcels of T-shirts, and posters rolled up like white shiny spying-glasses, and there is music from the man playing a set of drums, a tune I do not recognize, but full of pounding; he is the only man, the only person who can see and hear the invisible musicians accompanying him; and this music takes me all the way to where I can see the bridge, the underpass, although no one walks above my head. And the palm of the street which fans out and leads you either out of the city or else to the edge of the land, to the edge of the water. In summer, this street is filled with different colours of dress and of skin. And the screaming children rush and push their parents out of the way to board the ferry which takes them to an island small as a dot in the short distance from the mainland in the Lake. This island is not my island. I can only stand beside the end of the land and watch them, screaming for the lesser pleasure, the lesser beauty of this island dropped between the city and the Lake . . . this island is ugly compared to mine. For when I walked this distance yesterday, when it was also cold, the island was a mere trace in the mist that falls at the end of the land, at the beginning of the water.

John must have reached the hospital by now. I imagine him sitting on a metal chair, sitting with his shoulders hunched, and his cigar tapping the metal ashtray, waiting for the final tying of the invisible strings that sew up the wound; and he is sitting in his expensive winter coat, with his hat still on, and his tie loosened as men who work in offices loosen their ties to give the impression of work and mental concentration; and his woman, the child's mother, is pounding the corridor farther along the freshly waxed slippery dangerous tiles; or as a braver parent, she is on another floor over him, listening to her son's breathing, holding her son's hand. I imagine her counting each step, counting with each step the risks in the slicing of her son's body, to find the cancer perhaps . . . to find the germ, to find the growth that will continue to grow until it devours the entire small body of this child,

Rashid, made from love, if the knife does not cut it out. And I see her, up and down in a continual march, soft and almost silent, and with a cup of coffee in her hand, to stay awake, to see this child pass through the worst. But John is probably stuck to his seat in the strange, large, brightly lit room, waiting beside the ashtrays. This kind of wait is not meant to put a man at ease, or to sleep, even though the silent nurses ignore his anxiety which they are trained to face and detect. How many cigars has he taken out, placed to his lips, sucked on, and then refused to light? How much longer will he have to sit in the untalking Recovery room?

The water here is still green and dirty, and cold. There is no reflection in it now. There are no lights burning, neither from the restaurants nearby nor from the windows of the hotel and the apartments which rise on both my sides like lighthouses in the daytime. There is a speck of light moving across the water. It is like the fishing boat with the red sail, in a slice across the blue waves. And then it is not seen, as I wipe the rheum from the cold wind out of my eyes. I suddenly feel the urge to like this darkened scenery, this dimness, this cold water. I can get to love it, can embrace it like the water in summer or the waves on a beach, coming up to my feet over the sprawling pink sand. I can learn to feel there is no difference between the water, this Lake and that warm water of the blue sea.

Nothing is moving now. There are no cars. There are no trucks. No ambulances cry out. The machine that cleans the snow is not operating. The security guard who is to watch this unoccupied building cold and strong as granite, and as secure, is sleeping off his waking hours in which he caught no intruders. And the wooden seats are now like slabs of marble in the cemetery where she lies comfortable and asleep with her sprig of flower in her lap, just as she held her left hand in the crux of her thighs. They say it is warmer the farther down you go, even in this cold time; they say there is no difference that the dead can discern between themselves and those who are alive. The lives we live, passing our time in the warmer graves on the face of the land they say are just like death; they say you start to die the moment you reach forty; but I do not know if this is true for I do not any longer know anyone who is only forty. For when she passed away she was thirty and that was not a fair death, not a natural dying. It was a mistake and a tragedy. I have since quarrelled with God about His justice. And I have become mean-spirited over it.

John is standing now, with his arms outstretched and extended, creaking the fatigue out of his body. The colour of the skies is changing from the heavy weight of black to a more bearable dark blue, and I can feel my body getting cold and stiff. I think of John. I find myself imagining he cannot leave. That something has gone wrong. This fills me with hope. I see him sitting there, killing the boredom of waiting and the fear of the results of the knife the surgeon passes over the diagnosed parts of his son's body. I have been standing here longer than the time it takes my uncle to pass the knife sharpened on stone across the fat belly of the dolphin where the skin is whiter and less pink than on the flat sides. John is standing again, following the red seconds of the long hand of the electric clock that is moving in endless circles, moving through time. I pray that something will go wrong to keep him always here. I pray, and do not feel the pinch of guiltiness. Death has done this . . . I can see the shape of trees now, bursting through the greyish skies, across the Lake on the island. I hear the sounds of the breaking dawn, and can remember how they summon life, when once I was in hospital on another island: enamel hitting the iron posts, and screams . . . A truck stops behind me, and a man walking in the snow with a ballast of fresh bread in a green plastic milk case places it in confidence on the cold front step of the nearby restaurant. He leaves with greater confidence. No one in this city steals this kind of delivery. The light is silver-grey, and the water is still green and oily and not moving. I have been standing here now, with the metal railing guarding me from jumping in. The cold metal has no effect upon my comfort. With the Lake at my feet, at my beck and call, with the face of Lang in my mind, I am still here more hours than I have ever stood in one place.

The light is still not light enough to see too far, and the night is still; and noises – rats returning from the basement of the restaurant, the pounding of an early jogger foolish at this time, to brave this kind of weather, lands heavy on his heels and his passing resounds and vibrates along the metal rail, and I follow his pilgrim's progress until his exercise is succeeded by the opening of a garage door.

I hear the footsteps increasing in sound behind me, and I do not move or look to make sure I am safe. It may only be the guard roused by the coming of light. And because it is always so still, so peaceful, and so comfortable by the Lake, I have no need to save myself, or crave trials to find the reason. I can stand at this cold metal bar and watch the Lake, and see described in the dirty water her face that turns the water crystal. An object bobs on the surface, and I see that it is a flower . . .

Footsteps are behind me, pausing for certainty of courage and for clarity of direction, perhaps for caution, to be sure that the steps are approaching the right victim. I can almost hear the footsteps causing heavy breathing, as a man breathes before he is about to deliver a deadly blow. My body does not echo the anxiety in the approaching steps.

In the middle of the Lake is an inner tube drifting slowly upon the oil-spilled surface, in my direction; and I lean over like a man about to toss crumbs into the water to attract fish and ducks or the ugly birds which squeak and eat anything that is thrown to them.

The footsteps stop. And I can see the vapour from the person behind me come curling to reach the side of my face, and then come in front of me; and after this warning of attack or of approach, after this warning of arrival, I feel a touch upon my winter coat, as if someone is asking for my attention, or is asking for direction. John is dead in my wish of personal cruelty and selfishness. A light touch. A touch so certain and at the same time so much like a kiss, like Lang's kiss, that I can wait and relish its ecstasy. I do not have to wish for miracles any more, I have only to wait for the placing of the right hand on my right thigh, in our position of falling asleep without love-making. And then instead of her fragrance, I can smell the heavy, strong smell of cigar smoke, like the rising of smoke from the morning breakfast. The room is warm, and the bed is strewn with flowers, white flowers in the pattern of the cotton sheets; and the corridor is quiet, for the heavy woman is no longer walking outside the room in which a child lies breathing without tubes, for there was accuracy in the surgeon's knife; and six floors beneath her, as if in the deepness of an unfilled grave, the man who had been sitting beside the pile of smoked and unsmoked cigars can now stretch his limbs in a different manner, for it is success. It has been success, success at the heavy catch which fills the fishing boat, leaving only two inches from its brim before overflowing, and from giving back to the sea the hard-earned bountiful rewards of the sea; and there are voices of women scrambling along the beach, their anxiousness deeper than the marks of crabs which scamper from such pleasure and laughter; and the old black, patched inner tube, shining in the coming light, swirls and comes in, comes in in a rounding movement; and the hand is on my shoulder for a second time. This time it has more weight.

"He's alive," I say.

"Goddamn!"

This is all the voice says.